easy
Adobe® Premiere® Elements 2
Carl Plumer

Y0-AGW-703

Contents

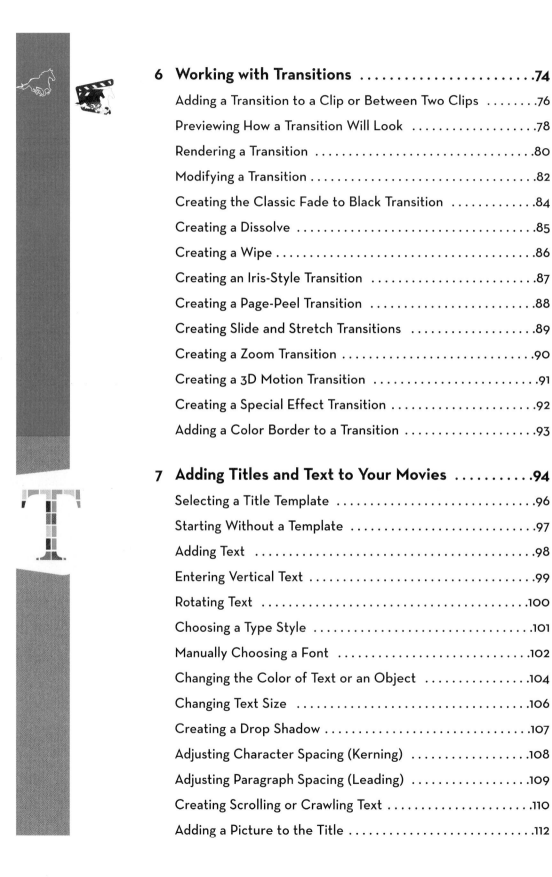

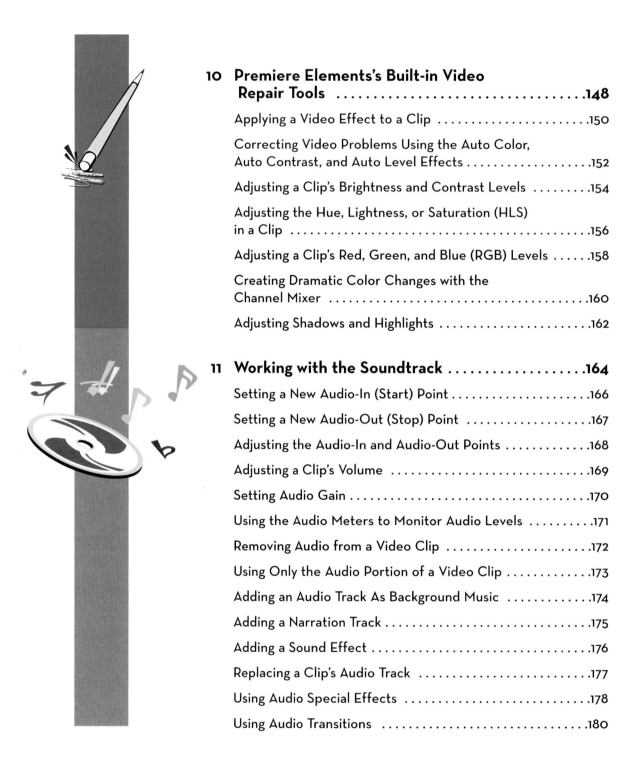

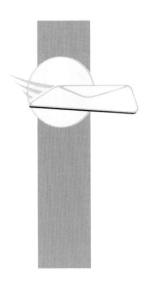

EASY ADOBE® PREMIERE® ELEMENTS 2

International Standard Book Number: 0-7897-3407-9

U.K. International Standard Book Number: 0-7897-3528-8

Library of Congress Catalog Card Number: 2005905790

Printed in the United States of America

First Printing: October 2005

08   07   06   05   4   3   2   1

TRADEMARKS

WARNING AND DISCLAIMER

BULK SALES

Que Publishing offers excellent discounts on this book when ordered in quantity for bulk purchases or special sales. For more information, please contact

U.S. Corporate and Government Sales

1-800-382-3419

corpsales@pearsontechgroup.com

For sales outside of the U.S., please contact

International Sales

international@pearsoned.com

Associate Publisher
Greg Wiegand

Acquisitions Editor
Laura Norman

Development Editor
Laura Norman

Managing Editor
Charlotte Clapp

Project Editor
Tonya Simpson

Production Editor
Heather Wilkins

Indexer
Aaron Black

Technical Editor
Amy Hoy

Publishing Coordinator
Sharry Lee Gregory

Interior Designer
Anne Jones

Cover Designer
Anne Jones

ABOUT THE AUTHOR

Carl Plumer is the desktop video guide for About.com, a division of the *New York Times*. He writes regularly about desktop video editing in general and Adobe Premiere Elements in particular. His site is consistently ranked among the top sites for desktop video and has regular readers from around the world. You can visit Carl's website at http://desktopvideo.about.com.

DEDICATION

To Kristen, my constant inspiration and without whom this book never would have been written: You amaze me every day with how wonderful you are! And to the best video subjects I could ever imagine: Joseph, Kira, Davis, and Hannah. I love you all.

ACKNOWLEDGMENTS

I want to first and foremost thank my editor, Laura Norman, for suggesting that I write this book and then guiding me through this amazing process. I want to also thank Tonya Simpson, Heather Wilkins, Amy Hoy, and everyone at Que who worked so hard to make sure this book came out right. And thanks, too, to the folks at About.com for allowing me to participate in that great virtual world of experts.

WE WANT TO HEAR FROM YOU!

As the reader of this book, *you* are our most important critic and commentator. We value your opinion and want to know what we're doing right, what we could do better, what areas you'd like to see us publish in, and any other words of wisdom you're willing to pass our way.

As an associate publisher for Que, I welcome your comments. You can email or write me directly to let me know what you did or didn't like about this book—as well as what we can do to make our books better.

Please note that I cannot help you with technical problems related to the topic of this book. We do have a User Services group, however, where I will forward specific technical questions related to the book.

When you write, please be sure to include this book's title and author as well as your name, email address, and phone number. I will carefully review your comments and share them with the author and editors who worked on the book.

Email: feedback@quepublishing.com

Mail: Greg Wiegand
          Associate Publisher
          Que Publishing
          800 East 96th Street
          Indianapolis, IN 46240 USA

For more information about this book or another Que title, visit our website at www.quepublishing.com. Type the ISBN (excluding hyphens) or the title of a book in the Search field to find the page you're looking for.

IT'S AS EASY AS 1-2-3

Each part of this book is made up of a series of short, instructional lessons, designed to help you understand basic information.

1 Each step is fully illustrated to show you how it looks onscreen.

2 Each task includes a series of quick, easy steps designed to guide you through the procedure.

3 Items that you select or click in menus, dialog boxes, tabs, and windows are shown in **bold**.

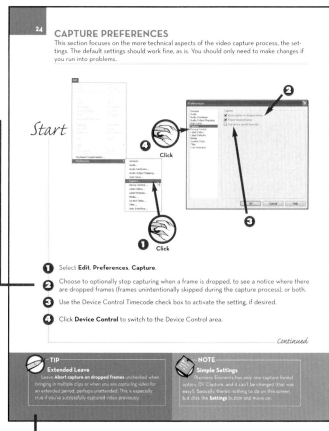

CAPTURE PREFERENCES

This section focuses on the more technical aspects of the video capture process, the settings. The default settings should work fine, as is. You should only need to make changes if you run into problems.

Start

1 Select **Edit**, **Preferences**, **Capture**.

2 Choose to optionally stop capturing when a frame is dropped, to see a notice where there are dropped frames (frames unintentionally skipped during the capture process), or both.

3 Use the Device Control Timecode check box to activate the setting, if desired.

4 Click **Device Control** to switch to the Device Control area.

Continued

TIP
Extended Leave
Leave **Abort capture on dropped frames** unchecked when bringing in multiple clips or when you are capturing video for an extended period, perhaps unattended. This is especially true if you've successfully captured video previously.

NOTE
Simple Settings
Premiere Elements has only one capture format option, DV Capture, and it can't be changed (that was easy!). Basically, there's nothing to do on this screen but click the **Settings** button and move on.

Drag

How to Drag:
Point to the starting place or object. Hold down the mouse button (right or left per instructions), move the mouse to the new location, then release the button.

Click

Tips, notes, and cautions give you a heads-up for any extra information you may need while working through the task.

Click:
Click the left mouse button once.

Keyboard

Click & Type:
Click once where indicated and begin typing to enter your text or data.

Selection:
Highlights the area onscreen discussed in the step or task.

Double-click:
Click the left mouse button twice in rapid succession.

Right-click:
Click the right mouse button once.

Pointer Arrow:
Highlights an item on the screen you need to point to or focus on in the step or task.

INTRODUCTION

When you write a story, you make a number of creative decisions as you go: what and who to write about; which scene should come first and which scenes next; and what, ultimately, has to be cut. Each decision you make helps your story flow and makes it a more satisfying experience for the reader.

Making a movie is the visual equivalent of that process. Like writing, your goal when making a movie is to tell a story. But this time, instead of using the written word, you're using images and sounds. And because the best video editors share something in common with the best writers—they don't get in the way of the story—the video editor knows that less is more, and that understatement, subtlety, and simplicity are best.

The tools that Premiere Elements provides to help you assemble your story pieces (the video clips) into a finished story (your movie) are some of the best available for the home video editor. After you have mastered Premiere Elements, you will find its working environment fits your video-editing tasks as nicely as your word processor fits your writing tasks. You can do virtually anything you have the creative vision for. And this book will teach you how.

Easy Adobe Premiere Elements 2 shows you the Easy way to make a movie using Premiere Elements 2. You'll discover how to bring your video clips into Premiere Elements and how to add photographs, titles, and music to your production. You'll learn how to add a special effect and toss in a transition. And don't worry if words such as *special effect* and *transition* sound foreign—they won't be for long.

So, congratulations: You're on your way to becoming a great movie editor in your own right. Step one was purchasing Adobe Premiere Elements. Step two was picking up *Easy Adobe Premiere Elements 2*!

INTRODUCING PREMIERE ELEMENTS 2

Premiere Elements 2 is without a doubt the most powerful entry-level video editor on the market. It is a direct descendent of one of the most respected names in the game, Adobe Premiere Pro, and as such, it contains many of the very same functions, effects, and controls as Premiere Pro. In fact, the two products are so similar that most of the plug-ins (third party add-ons, such as additional filters and special effects) that were created for Premiere Pro should work with Premiere Elements, too.

You'll find after you play around with Premiere Elements a bit and become more comfortable with using it that Premiere Elements is not only powerful and capable of doing almost everything a video editor needs her software to do, it is also remarkably easy to use—especially after reading this book. While other software gives you one or maybe two video tracks to work with, Premiere Elements gives you 99. And while you might never use 99 tracks, or even more than 5 or 6, it's good to know that Premiere Elements has that kind of support. With virtually unlimited tracks, you can create many of the effects the big studios do. If you're familiar with the television show *24*, you'll know how they have many scenes playing in small windows on the screen at once. You've seen this effect in recent movies, as well. No other consumer video-editing software enables you to re-create this *24* effect other than Premiere Elements! The reason is, Premiere Elements has multiple video tracks, each one of which can be a picture-in-picture (PiP).

Not only does Premiere Elements give you the ability to create impressive special effects such as zooming in on your clips or panning across a photograph (known as the Ken Burns effect), but Premiere Elements also has excellent filters for correcting common video and lighting problems such as undersaturated colors, or clips that are too dark, or that have a hum in the audio track. Premiere Elements enables you to run clips backward, speed them up, change the sound of people's voices, or switch out one audio track for another.

Premiere Elements does all this (and considerably more) with a user interface that is actually fun to use. If you are new to Premiere Elements, stay with the basics: capture, basic editing, and export (save to file or DVD). Premiere Elements will work like a charm and you will feel like a video genius!

PREMIERE ELEMENTS: YOUR VIDEO-EDITING STUDIO

Premiere Elements is a professional video-editing studio in your computer.

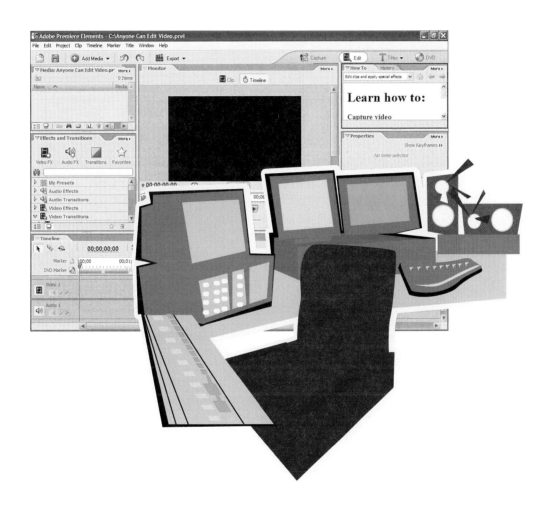

STARTING PREMIERE ELEMENTS

When you start Premiere Elements, you first see the welcome screen. Here you can choose from a number of options. By the way, if you ever want to return to the welcome screen and Premiere Elements is already running, just select **File**, **New**, **Project**, **Cancel** and it magically appears!

Double-Click

 Start

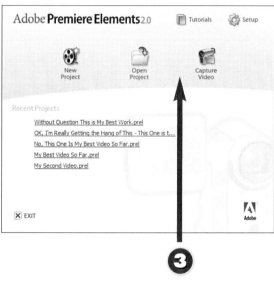

1 Double-click the **Premiere Elements 2.0 icon** on your desktop, or select **Start**, **All Programs**, **Adobe**, **Adobe Premiere Elements 2.0**.

2 The Premiere Elements splash screen displays.

3 This is followed by the Premiere Elements welcome screen. Here you can select to start a new project, open an existing project, or go directly to capturing video for a new project.

 End

-TIP-
The Latest Projects List
Premiere Elements keeps track of the most recent projects you worked on in a list on the opening screen. If the project you want is not on this list, just click the **Open Project** button to browse your computer for it.

-TIP-
All This and More...
Although almost every time you start Premiere Elements you will be choosing from the three choices discussed in the steps, you can also load tutorial project files, access setup screens, go to Adobe's website, and exit the program.

STARTING A NEW PROJECT

When you start a new project in Premiere Elements, you simply give your project a name and tell Premiere Elements where you want to store the project files on your computer.

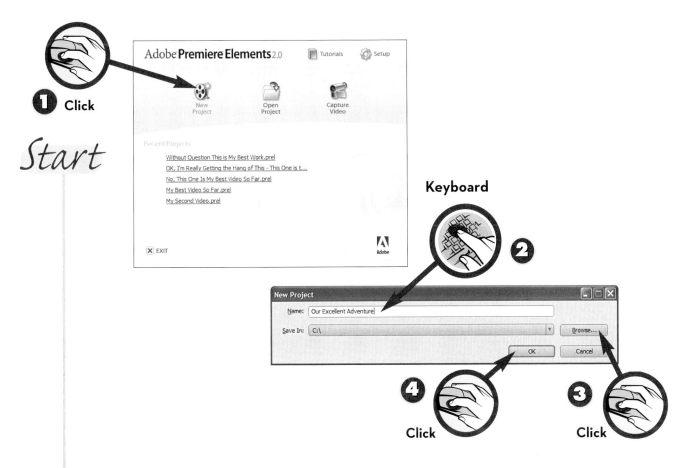

Start

End

1. On the Premiere Elements opening screen, click the **New Project** button.

2. Type a name in the **Project Name** field in the New Project dialog box.

3. Click the **Browse** button to look for a location for the project files or use the drop-down menu to select from the last few locations you saved in.

4. Click **OK**. Premiere Elements loads and you're ready to go!

TIP

File This Under Tips

Two things: Be sure you have a *huge* hard drive for video editing, at least 80GB, but 120–200GB is ideal. Consider organizing your videos under a folder, perhaps called (strangely enough) Video Projects. Under that folder, save your Premiere Elements projects with informative names. For example, don't use Video Project 1. Instead use Our Trip to Orlando Florida in Summer 2006 with Stopover at Uncle Eddie's Bungalow in the Keys or a happy medium between the two, but you get the idea...

OPENING AN EXISTING PROJECT

Anytime you open Premiere Elements with the intention of returning to a project already underway, you can select the project directly off the welcome screen if it was a recently active project, or use the **Open Project** button to look around for it on your hard drive if it has been awhile since you worked on it.

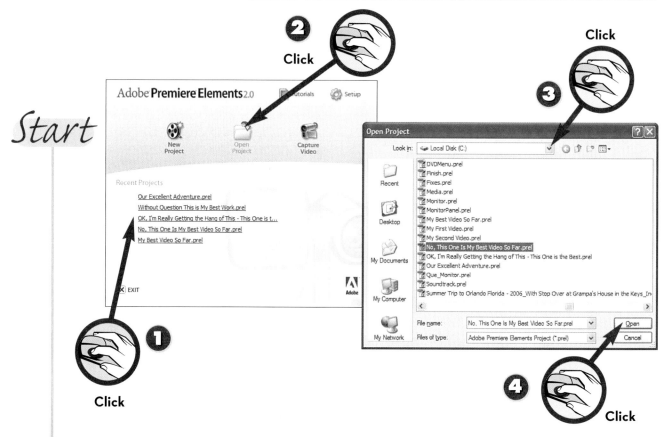

If the project you want to work on is listed on the welcome screen, click on it to load it into Premiere Elements.

Optionally, click the **Open Project** button to open the Browse dialog box.

Use the **Look In** drop-down in the Browse dialog box to find the project you want.

Click **Open**.

NOTE

About Organization

If you are well organized and use informative filenames, you will be able to quickly find the project you want. Create a folder called Video Projects. Under that folder, always store your Premiere Elements projects and give them clear, descriptive names.

TIP

File This Under Redundancy

That list of recently worked-on projects you can choose from on the Premiere Elements opening screen? It's the exact same list of projects you'll find under **File**, **Open Recent Projects**.

TWO SUPERSTARS: THE MONITOR AND TIMELINE

After you start Premiere Elements and are looking at the interface, two components stand out most prominently and are perhaps the two areas in Premiere Elements that you will be working with the most as you build your movie. These are the Monitor panel and the Timeline, the superstars, if you will, of Premiere Elements.

Start

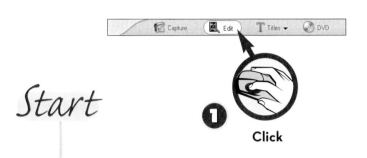

Click

1 Click the **Edit** button from the taskbar to display the Monitor panel and Timeline at their best.

2 The Monitor panel has controls similar to the controls on a remote control. It's here where you watch your clips and make your edit decisions.

3 The Timeline has rows (called *tracks*) for video (you can also place images and titles here) as well as audio. It's here where you actually build your movie.

End

-- NOTE --

For Your Viewing Pleasure

Unless you have installed some other software on your computer, if and when you export your video to a file such as a Windows media file (**.WMV**) or Apple QuickTime file (**.MOV**), you will watch your movie on your computer using either the Windows Media Player or the QuickTime Player.

THE PREMIERE ELEMENTS WORKSPACES

Premiere Elements uses the concept of workspaces to define the space you are working in based on the task. Although the interface doesn't change dramatically in most cases, the workspace will change to introduce a new window or other element. The four workspaces in Premiere Elements are the Capture workspace, the Edit workspace, the Titles workspace, and the DVD workspace.

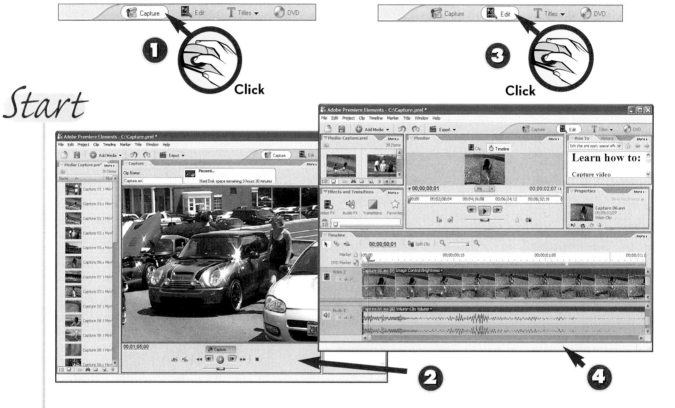

1 Click on the **Capture** button on the taskbar to view the Capture workspace.

2 The Capture panel has replaced the Monitor panel, and the Timeline and Effects palettes have disappeared. The Media panel has grown considerably, as has the Help panel.

3 Click on the **Edit** button to return to the Edit workspace.

4 Notice that the Monitor panel now replaces the Capture panel and the interface has returned to home; that is, to its most familiar state.

Continued

NOTE

Detailed Instructions

This book contains many steps and illustrations for both capturing video and editing it. You'll find that information in other parts of this book. Right now, we are just familiarizing ourselves with the look and operation of Premiere Elements.

TIP

"More" for Your Money

The More menu/button, available on the upper-right corner of every Premiere Elements panel, provides additional functionality. The More button is an integral part of the Premiere Elements interface: know it, use it, love it.

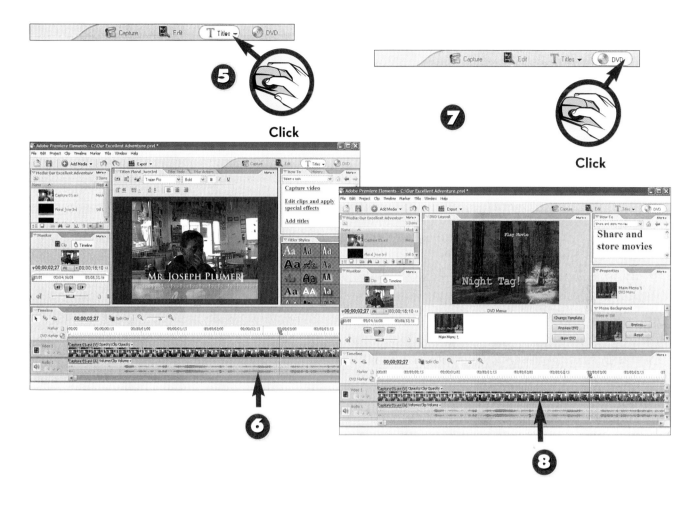

Click

Click

Click the **Titles** button to view the Titles workspace. (Click **Cancel** when the Templates window displays to close it.)

Click the **Titles** button to view the Titles workspace. (Click **Cancel** when the Templates window displays to close it.)

The Monitor panel shrunk and moved. And where it was, the Title Designer panel now sits. The Properties panel has now been replaced by the Titler Styles panel.

Click the **DVD** button to open the DVD workspace. (Click **Cancel** when the DVD Templates panel displays to close it.)

Notice that the Titles panel is replaced by the DVD Layout panel. The Capture panel and the interface has returned to home; that is, to its most familiar state.

End

TIP
Titles Mini-Menu
The Titles button menu includes options for opening the Title Templates panel, creating a new title, or creating a scrolling or crawling title. You'll find more information in Part 7, "Adding Titles and Text to Your Movies," **p. 94** of this book.

TIP
Button Groupings
Additional buttons on the taskbar are available on the left, grouped by function: Open Project and Save Project; Add Media; Undo/Redo; and Export Project.

CHANGING PANEL SIZES

You can adjust the size of an individual panel, such as the Monitor panel, as you require.
When you do so, all of the other panels resize to accommodate.

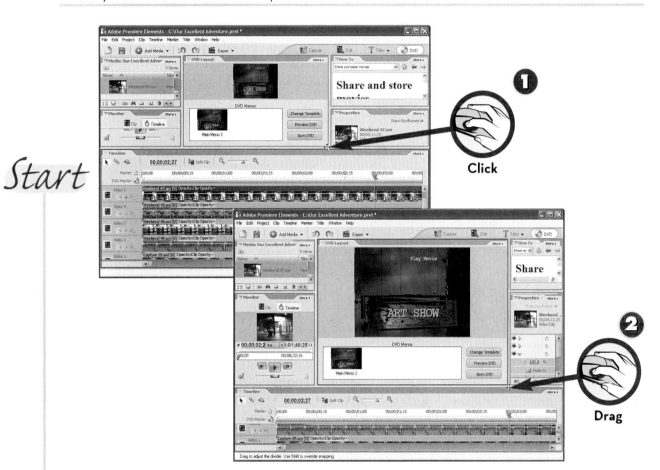

Start

Click

Drag

1 Click on a corner or side of the panel whose size or shape you want to change.

2 Click and drag the panel to a new size and/or shape.

End

NOTE

Resize Me

Notice that whatever size or shape you make the panel you're adjusting, all of the other panels in Premiere Elements resize themselves dynamically (in other words, they resize while you are resizing the panel) to fill the screen just right.

TIP

Restore Me

If you've rearranged everything into a mess, it's a snap to fix. Just select **Window**, **Restore Workspace** and select the workspace you want to fix—**Edit**, **Capture**, **Titles**, or **DVD**.

CUSTOMIZING THE PREMIERE ELEMENTS INTERFACE

Premiere Elements is 100% customizable. You can move the panels around on the screen by simply grabbing and dragging to a new spot. You can nest the panels together into a set of tabs. You can also move a panel from the bottom of the screen to the top, or move it to one side to the other to suit your working style.

Start

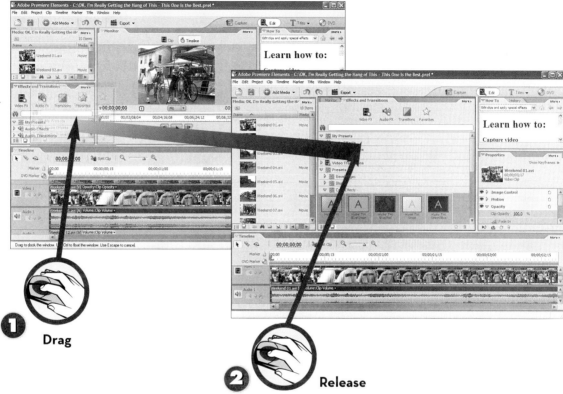

Drag

Release

① Drag the panel you want to relocate and move it across the screen. You'll see a copy of it ghost transparently along with your mouse as you move it.

② Release the mouse button to place the panel at that spot.

End

TIP

Dark or Light

Select **Edit**, **Preferences**, **User Interface** and use the slider to adjust the brightness. Select **Use Windows Background Color** to apply the default application colors to Premiere Elements's dialog boxes and certain other elements.

NOTE

Free Floating

As you pass over a candidate panel, a multipane box appears, showing you that you can safely drop the panel onto that spot. But be careful. Unless you want free-floating panels, don't drag a panel out of the interface.

SETTING PREFERENCES

Premiere Elements has a number of preference settings you can individualize, such as autosave timings and the color of the labels Premiere Elements uses for media types. It's here you set the drive to which Premiere Elements writes scratch files. If you have a preference other than the default Premiere Elements chooses (such as a larger external hard drive, for example), you can change it. For most of us, however, the settings on the Preferences screen are probably fine as is unless you have a specific need or circumstance.

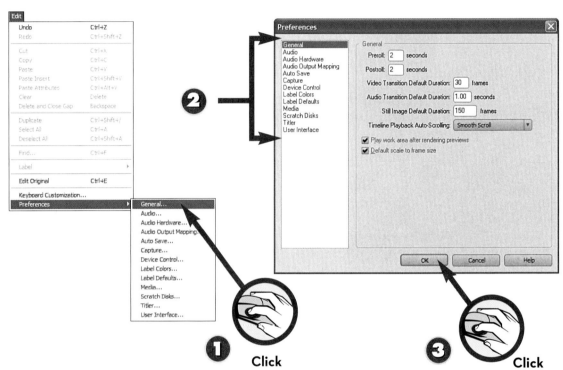

Click

Click

1. Select **Edit**, **Preferences**, **General** to access the Preferences screen.

2. Optionally, select from the list of preference areas along the left side of this screen to make modifications to any of the preference areas.

3. Click **OK**.

 TIP

Preferences, Preferences

The Preferences screen is actually 13 screens in one. You can access the individual preferences screens by clicking **Edit**, **Preferences** and then selecting just the preferences screen you want from the fly-out menu.

 TIP

Customizing the Keyboard

You might need to change a shortcut in Premiere Elements, perhaps because it conflicts with another program you're using. If so, just use **Edit**, **Keyboard Customization** to access the Keyboard Customization screen.

MODIFYING PROJECT SETTINGS

You can modify a number of project settings in Premiere Elements, including video and audio settings, capture settings, Timeline settings, and other settings. You probably won't need to make any changes to these settings until after you've experimented with Premiere Elements for a while, but it's still good to know the options are there when you are ready for them.

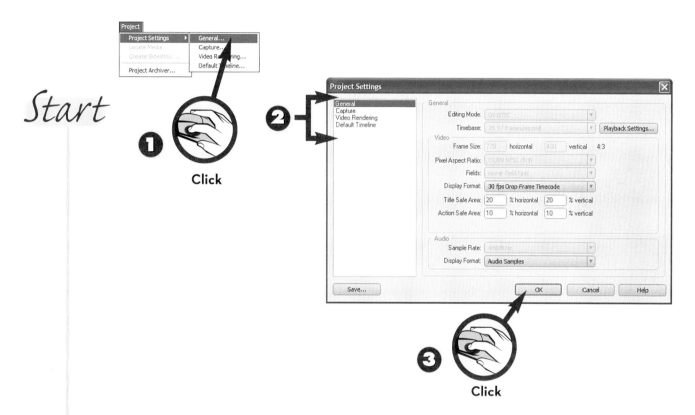

Start

Click

Click

End

1 Select **Project**, **Project Settings**, **General** to access the Project Settings screen.

2 Select from the list of project settings along the left side of the Project Settings screen to make modifications to any of the project settings areas.

3 Click **OK**.

TIP
Project Settings Screens
The Project Settings screen is actually four screens in one. You can access an individual project settings screen by selecting **Edit**, **Project Settings** and then selecting just the project settings screen you want from the menu.

TIP
Save Your Settings
If you make a significant number of changes across all four Project Settings screens, you might want to save your settings. To do so, click the **Save** button. Give the project settings a name and a description in the Save Projects Settings screen.

SAVING YOUR WORK

You can save your work at any time in three ways: normal Save, Save As, and Save a Copy.

Start

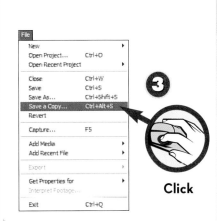

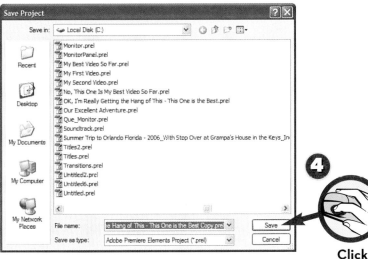

1 To save your work in progress, select **File**, **Save**.

2 To save your project as a new project and immediately *start working* in the *new* project, select **File**, **Save As**.

3 To save your project as a new project but *continue working* in the *same* project you were already working in, select **File**, **Save A Copy**.

4 Selecting **Save As** or **Save a Copy** presents you with the Save Project dialog. Give the project a name and click **Save**.

End

ARCHIVING YOUR PROJECT

Premiere Elements provides you with a tool for archiving your project so it's available to work in at some future date with all of the source files intact. At the bottom of the Project Archiver screen, Premiere Elements provides you with the size of the archive and the amount of available disk space on the currently selected hard drive to help you decide whether to locate the archive file elsewhere.

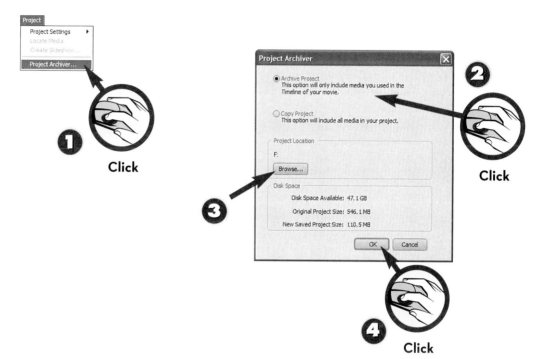

Start

Click

Click

Click

End

① Select **Project**, **Project Archiver**.

② On the Project Archiver screen, select to archive all media in the Media panel or just the media currently used on the Timeline.

③ Optionally, select a new drive and directory (folder) to store the archive file. Otherwise, Premiere Elements uses the current project folder.

④ Click **OK**.

NOTE

Archival Information

Archiving means simply filing away in a vault or library kind of way. If you simply save your project, there's a chance you might move video clips or sound files to another location, or even delete files. So, when you return next week, or perhaps next year, to make an updated version of your video, you run into problems. By working with the archive, all of your files are ready to go.

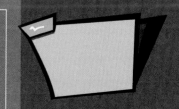

THE CAPTURE PANEL

The Capture panel's interface looks a bit like the LCD screen on your camcorder. With it, you review the video you took and select some or all of it to bring in to your computer. That way, you can get right down to the good part: editing your video project with Premiere Elements. So, get comfortable with the Capture panel and how to use it. It's an essential part of the video-editing process.

If your camera is a digital video (DV) camcorder, you can connect it directly to Premiere Elements by connecting a FireWire cable to your camera and your PC. Premiere Elements can then control your camera, and it enables you to select your movie scenes directly from your camera's media, rather than importing everything you recorded.

If you have an analog camcorder, the process isn't quite as simple, but you can still get the video you've recorded from your camera into your computer. To transfer the video to your computer, you'll need either a video capture card (in your computer) or an external analog-to-digital (A-D) converter box to plug your camcorder and computer into. Use the software that came with the capture card or A-D device to get your video onto your computer's hard drive. Back in Premiere Elements, use the Add Media button (see Part 3, "The Media Panel") to import your clips into Premiere Elements.

YOUR INTERFACE BETWEEN THE WORLD AND YOUR COMPUTER

The Capture panel is your interface between the video you take and the films you make.

Gather your footage out in the field...

...use the Capture panel to bring your video clips into your computer...

...and start editing!

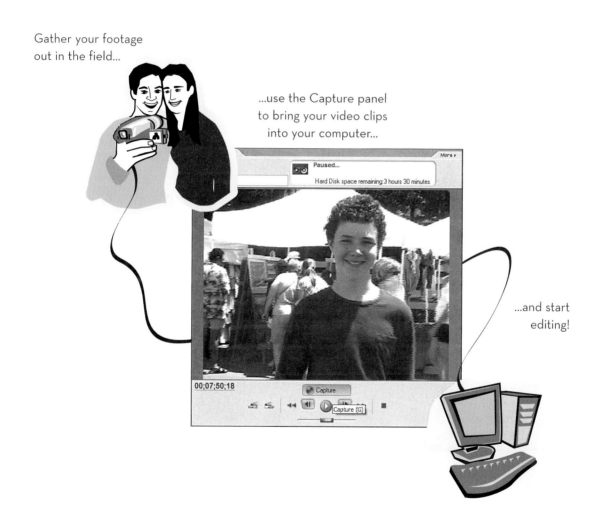

CONNECTING YOUR CAMCORDER TO PREMIERE ELEMENTS

The process of connecting your camcorder to your computer and setting Premiere Elements to recognize and control it is very straightforward. It will become second-nature to you in no time!

Start

Click

End

① Connect your FireWire cable to your camcorder's FireWire port.

② Connect the other end of the FireWire cable to your computer's FireWire port.

③ Turn your camcorder on to **PLAY** (or **VCR/VTR**).

④ Click the **Capture** button to open the Capture panel.

TIP
Where's the Picture?
If you don't see a picture in the Preview window, your capture settings might be set to not display a preview during the capture process. See "Reviewing the Default Capture Settings," **p. 22**, for instructions on changing this and other settings.

TIP
Where's My Device?
If the top button reads Capture Device Offline, Premiere Elements can't find your camcorder. Be sure your camcorder is turned on and is in PLAY/VCR mode. Check that your FireWire cables are snug at both ends.

SELECTING CAPTURE OPTIONS FROM THE MORE MENU

When you capture clips, you might want to capture just the video or just the audio, or you might want Premiere Elements to drop the clips onto the Timeline as they're captured. These settings are easy to access and change on the fly.

Start

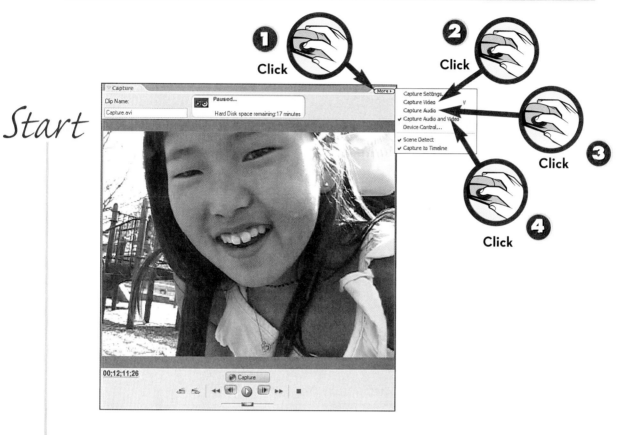

1 On the Capture panel, click the **More** button.

2 Choose **Capture Video** to capture *only* the video of a clip (clicking an option once selects and checks it; clicking it again unchecks it).

3 Choose **Capture Audio** to capture *only* the audio of a clip.

4 Click **Capture Audio and Video** to capture *both* the video and audio.

End

TIP
Scene Stealer
Choose **Scene Detect** on the More menu to find where you stopped and started recording. Premiere Elements saves them as separate clips. To determine your scenes manually, uncheck the **Scene Detect** option.

TIP
Good Timing
Leave the **Capture to Timeline** option unchecked. This way, your new clips are placed only in the Media panel so you can edit them first. If you want to automatically place incoming clips on to the Timeline, check this option.

CAPTURING VIDEO CLIPS

Premiere Elements uses device control technology to control your DV camcorder from your computer using VCR-like controls.

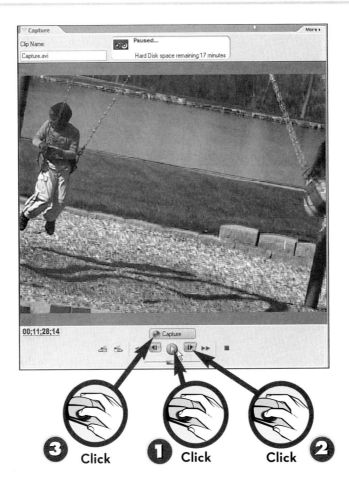

3 Click   **1** Click   **2** Click

1 Click the **Play** button to play the tape in the camcorder.

2 Navigate to the scene you want to capture using the navigation buttons at the bottom of the window (**Rewind, Step Back, Fast Forward, Step Forward, Previous Scene, Next Scene**).

3 When you have found a scene on the tape that you want to capture, click the **Capture** button.

Continued

TIP
Clear Signals
Keep an eye on the icon and message area at the top of the Capture panel. It tells you when the camcorder is in Play, Pause, or Fast-forward mode and so on. It also tells you how much space you have left on your hard drive (in terms of hours and minutes).

TIP
Timecode Trick
If you want to jump to a particular place on the tape, type the timecode into the timecode area to the left, just below the image. The timecode is in HH;MM;SS;FF (hours, minutes, seconds, frames) format.

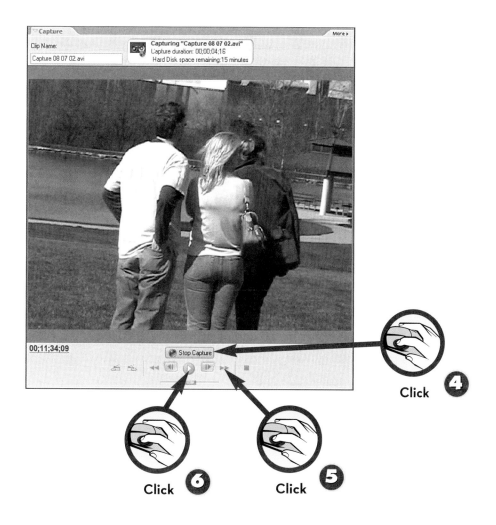

When you have finished capturing, click **Stop Capture**.

Navigate to the next scene you want to capture and repeat Steps 1, 2, 3, and 4 as needed.

Click the **Pause** button (the Play button becomes the Pause button) to pause the tape in the camcorder as needed.

End

NOTE

Easy Clip Capture

If you're using the **Scene Detect** option, you don't need to continually click **Capture/Stop Capture** because Premiere Elements divides the scenes automatically. The individual scenes are numbered consecutively, such as scene001.avi, scene002.avi, and so on.

TIP

Keyboard Options

Use the **Spacebar** on the keyboard to play and pause the camcorder and use the **J**, **K**, and **L** keys to fast reverse, pause, and fast forward, respectively.

REVIEWING THE DEFAULT CAPTURE SETTINGS

You can review or set your capture settings whenever you want. You will most likely change or set them only once, if at all, unless you buy a new camcorder.

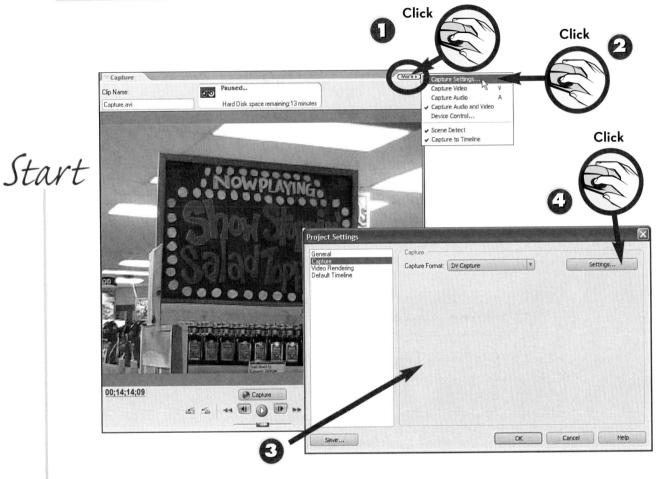

Start

Click ①

Click ②

Click ④

③

---

① On the Capture panel, click the **More** button.

② Click **Capture Settings**.

③ The **Project Settings** window shows the **Capture** options section.

④ Click the **Settings** button. Note that the Settings button will not display if your camcorder is not connected to your PC.

Continued

— NOTE —

Simple Settings

Premiere Elements has only one capture format option, DV Capture, and it can't be changed (that was easy!). Basically, there's nothing to do on this screen but click the **Settings** button and move on.

— NOTE —

Second Avenue

You can also get to this Project Settings window by selecting **Project** from the Premiere Elements menu bar, and then selecting **Project Settings, Capture**.

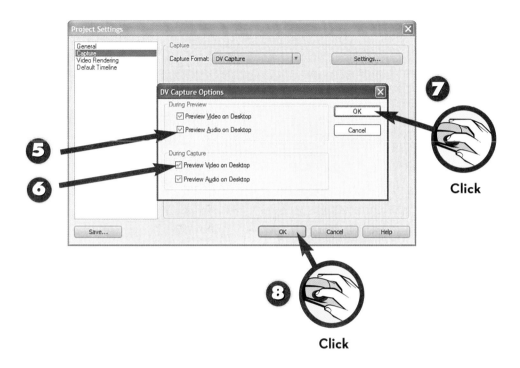

Click

Click

5 On the DV Capture Options dialog, choose whether to play the video and/or audio on your computer screen while simultaneously previewing your video.

6 Choose whether to preview the video and audio onscreen when capturing from the DV camera.

7 Click **OK** to exit the DV Capture Options dialog and save your choices (click Cancel to exit without saving).

8 Click **OK** to exit the Project Settings window and return to the Capture panel.

End

TIP
Capturing Your Share of Problems
If you have problems capturing video clips, come back to the DV Capture Options dialog and uncheck **Preview Video on Desktop** or **Preview Audio on Desktop**, or both. If your computer is a bit slow for the task or has less than the ideal amount of RAM, shutting off these preview functions can free up the CPU and some RAM that might make for successful video capture.

CAPTURE PREFERENCES

This section focuses on the more technical aspects of the video capture process, the settings. The default settings should work fine, as is. You should only need to make changes if you run into problems.

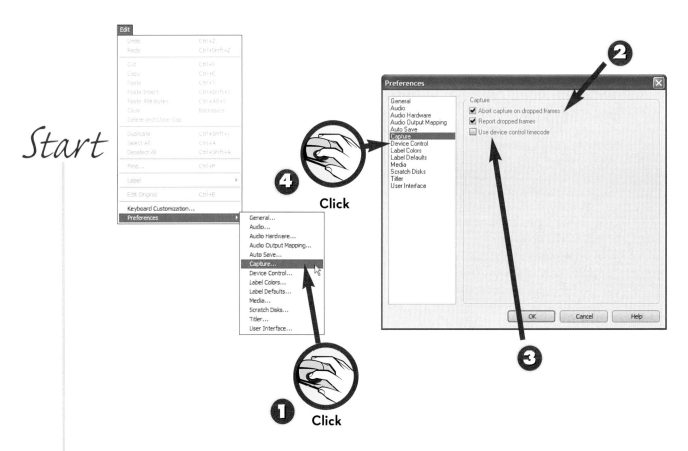

Start

Click

Click

1 Select **Edit**, **Preferences**, **Capture**.

2 Choose to optionally stop capturing when a frame is dropped, to see a notice where there are dropped frames (frames unintentionally skipped during the capture process), or both.

3 Use the Device Control Timecode check box to activate the setting, if desired.

4 Click **Device Control** to switch to the Device Control area.

Continued

TIP
Extended Leave
Leave **Abort capture on dropped frames** unchecked when bringing in multiple clips or when you are capturing video for an extended period, perhaps unattended. This is especially true if you've successfully captured video previously.

TIP
Don't Panic
If you discover that you have a clip with dropped frames, don't immediately recapture the clip. View the clip first. The frames might be from a section of the clip you weren't intending on using in your finished project anyway. Problem solved!

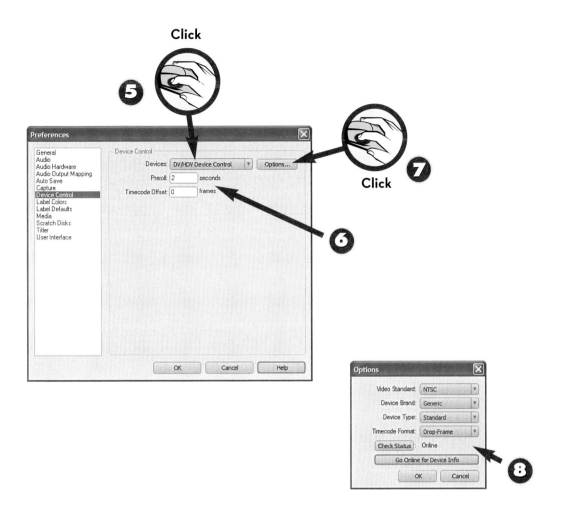

Click

Click

The default is for **DV/HDV Device Control**. Leave it as is unless you are using a USB Video Class 1.0 device; in which case, select that option.

The **Preroll** and **Timecode Offset** areas are very rarely changed. Adjusting these settings might help, however, if you have trouble capturing clips from your camcorder.

Click **Options** to open the DV Device Control Options window.

Set camcorder device information as needed, and click **OK**.

End

TIP

Scratch It

The **Scratch Disks** area of the Preferences screen is where you select the drives and folders for Premiere Elements to store captured video and audio clips. You actually don't have to change Premiere Elements' defaults for any of the scratch disk locations; you can just go with the settings as is. The only time you might consider changing these scratch disks is if you have a second large hard drive that you want to specify for use as your video and audio capture drive.

THE MEDIA PANEL

The Premiere Elements Media panel is the place where you add and store the various clips you plan to use in your production. The Media panel is a sophisticated panel that has numerous features to help you stay organized, gather your media, analyze your media's properties, and quickly get to work creating your video. The Premiere Elements Media panel is intended to be customized, but you can work with it exactly as shipped, without ever customizing a single thing. When you capture video from a camcorder (see Part 2, "The Capture Panel"), the clip or clips you capture are added to the Media panel automatically and they can optionally be added to the Timeline as well.

You can add any type of clip that is supported by Premiere Elements from your hard drive or DVD drive, including video clips, still images, titles, music files, sound effects, and more. Premiere Elements' Media panel supports the following file formats:

Video:

AVI, MPEG/MPE/MPG, MOV, and WMV

Pictures:

BMP, EPS, GIF, ICO, JPEG, JPG, PDD, PDF, PNG, PSD, and TIFF

Audio:

AIFF, AVI, MOV, MP3, WAV, and WMA

This list of file formats might not mean a whole lot to you right now, but after you've spent a little time working with your media clips you'll find it very useful to know with which formats Premiere Elements can and can't work.

COLLECT, ORGANIZE, AND TRACK YOUR CLIPS

The Media panel is a painter's palette of media clips, awaiting your creative inspiration.

ADDING MEDIA FROM YOUR HARD DRIVE

You can add any type of media supported by Premiere Elements to your production that you have available on your hard drive.

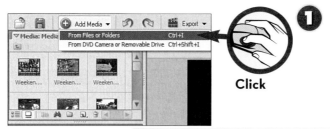

Click

Start

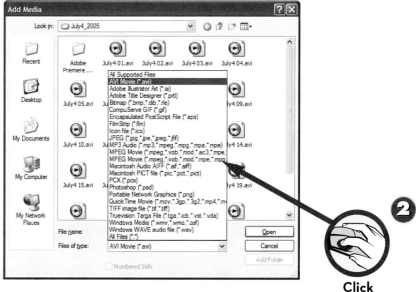

Click

1 Click the **Add Media** button (you can also select **File, Add Media)** and select **From Files or Folders**.

2 By default, Premiere Elements is set to recognize any and all of its supported file types, but you can narrow your search by selecting from the drop-down list in the **Files of Type** field.

Continued

TIP

Keyboard Method
The quick keyboard way to add media from your hard drive is to press **Control-I**. This is the same as selecting the **Add Media** button and then selecting **From Files and Folders**.

Click

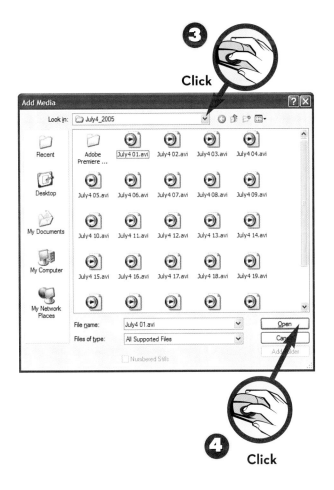

Click

---

3 Browse through other folders by clicking the drop-down arrow next to the **Look In** field.

4 Click to select the file (or Ctrl+click to select multiple files) you want to add to the Media panel and click **Open**.

End

TIP

Multiple-file Magic

You can add an entire folder of media to Premiere Elements at one time. To do so, browse to a folder, select it, and click the **Add Folder** button. The contents of the folder are added to Premiere Elements, along with the compatible files in any subfolders.

ADDING MEDIA FROM REMOVABLE MEDIA OR A REMOVABLE DRIVE

You can add media from your CD or DVD drive or supported removable drive, or even from your DVD camera directly into Premiere Elements in just a few steps using the Media Downloader.

Start

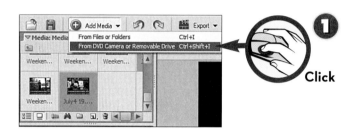

Click

① Click the **Add Media** button (you can also select **File**, **Add Media)** and select **From DVD Camera or Removable Drive**.

Continued

TIP

Room for a View

Use the slider at the bottom of the window to zoom in closer to see more detail, or zoom out to see more of the thumbnails. Use the scrollbar as needed to see more available files. To view files by type, use the **Show** buttons at the top left of the window.

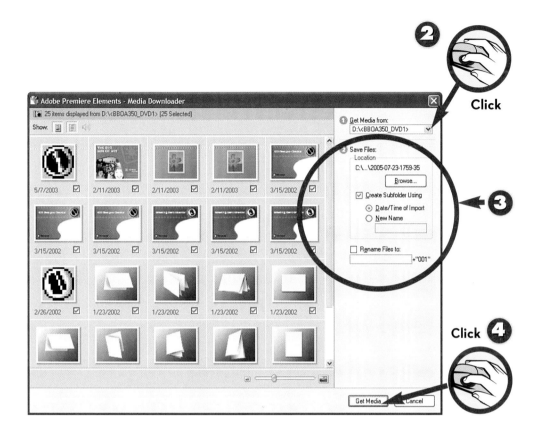

2 Select the media source from the Media Downloader.

3 Choose your save options and select the media you want to use. Be sure to uncheck any media that you don't want to use.

4 Click the **Get Media** button to add your selected media to your project.

End

TIP

Copy It Right
While Premiere Elements gives you access to all sorts of media with the Media Downloader, it won't let you copy any media on a copy-protected drive or disc.

SWITCHING VIEWS

Premiere Elements gives you a number of ways to set up the Media panel so you can access your clips the way you like. You might find that the way you like changes from project to project or even from minute to minute. Here's how to set up the Media panel for List view.

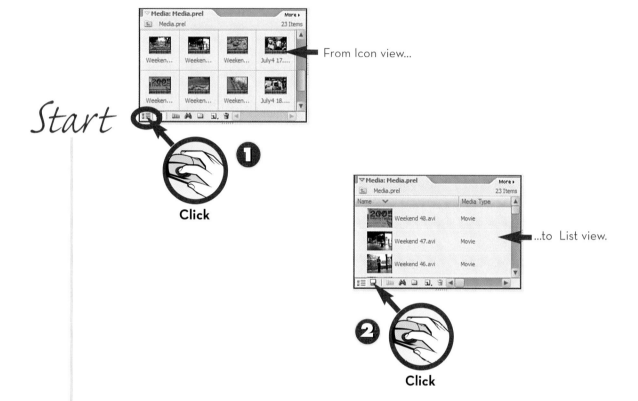

Start

Click

From Icon view...

...to List view.

Click

1 Click the **List** button (or select the Media panel's **More** menu and then click **View, List**).

2 Click the **Icon** button to return to Icon view.

End

VIEWING MEDIA INFORMATION

Working in List view enables you to control how much information you want to access about the clips you add to a project. Certain projects might require you to view the time-code, for example, or a media clip's description or notes.

Start

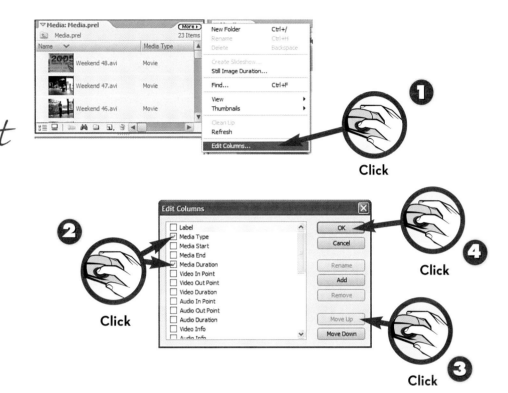

Click

Click

Click

Click

1. Click on the Media panel's **More** menu and then click **Edit Columns**.

2. Click in the checkboxes for any column you want to see from the list in the **Edit Columns** window.

3. Optionally use the **Move Up** and **Move Down** buttons to adjust the order of your columns, as needed.

4. Click **OK**.

End

ADDING COMMENTS AND DESCRIPTIONS TO MEDIA

Working in List view enables you to control how much information you want to access about the clips you add to a project. If you use the Edit Columns window to add editable fields, you can enter comments and descriptions to help you keep track of what your clips contain.

Start

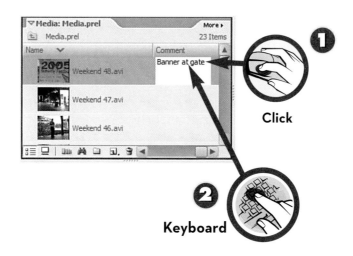

Click

Keyboard

1 Click in any editable field for a clip, such as **Comment** or **Description**.

2 Enter text as needed.

End

CLEANING UP THE MEDIA PANEL IN ICON VIEW

Clean Up is useful for getting rid of blank spaces in the Media panel without having to drag all of your clips around to fill the empty spaces.

Start

Click

The Media panel in disarray...

The Media panel, Zen

1 Click the Media panel's **More** menu.

2 Choose **Clean Up**.

End

-TIP-
Dude, Where's My Clip?
Clean Up is also a useful function to use anytime you've resized the Media panel and clips are now no longer visible. Selecting **More**, **Clean Up** realigns all clips so more of them show in the Media panel as it is currently sized.

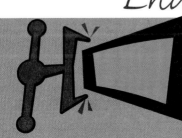

USING THE PREVIEW AREA FOR A QUICK LOOK AT A CLIP

Use Preview to take a quick peek at any video clip to view the contents without having to load it into the Monitor window.

Start

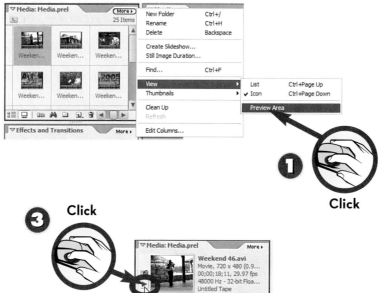

Click

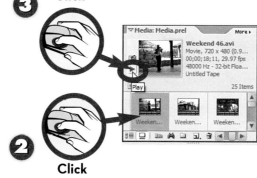

Click

Click

1 Activate the Preview area by selecting **More**, **View**, **Preview Area**.

2 Select the media you want to view. It loads into the Preview area.

3 Click the mini **Play** button just to the left of the Preview area to play the clip. (Click again to stop the clip.)

End

NOTE

Preview Information, Too

The Preview area also quickly supplies you with additional information about your clips. As you click through the clips in the Media panel, you'll see the name of the file and the type of file listed just to the right of the Preview area's poster frame for the clip. If it's a video clip, you'll see its size; whether it is used in your project (and how many times); its duration (in timecode format); and the frames per second (fps). It will also show you audio information and the name of the tape it came from.

SETTING THE CLIP'S POSTER FRAME

The first frame of a clip doesn't always give a good indication of what a clip is about. Premiere Elements uses the first frame of the clip as the poster frame to display in the Preview area, but you can select a different frame so you have a much better idea of what the clip contains when you are viewing your clips in the Media panel.

Start

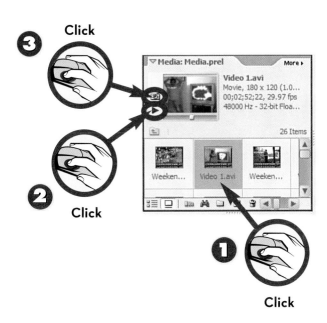

Click

Click

Click

① Select the clip you want to view to load it into the Preview area.

② Click the mini **Play** button in the Preview area to play the clip.

③ When you see a scene that you'd like to use as the poster, click the mini **Poster Frame** button (it looks like a little camera).

End

TIP

Preview All

All clips load into the Preview area, not just video clips. But only files with animation or sound are played in the Preview window. By the way, be sure the Preview window is active by selecting the **More** button on the Media panel and then selecting **View**, **Preview Area**.

ORGANIZING CLIPS ON THE MEDIA PANEL

In Icon view, you can move clips around to get them in the order you need for your project by dragging and dropping them anywhere you want.

Start

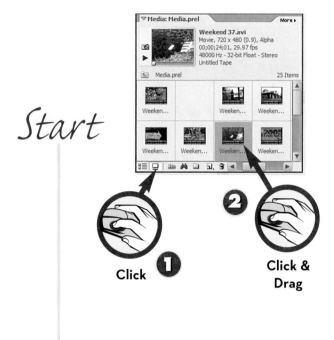

Click ①

Click & Drag ②

Click ③

① Switch to **Icon view**, if you aren't already in it.

② Click and drag on a clip to drag it anywhere, including into a folder or subfolder.

③ Optionally click on the **Delete** button (the little garbage can at the bottom of the Media panel) to remove it from the project.

End

TIP
Making Copies
To duplicate a clip, you can use **Copy** and **Paste**, and you can also right-click (or select **Edit** from the Premiere Elements menu), and choose **Duplicate**.

TIP
Safe Delete
When you delete any clip from the Media panel or from anywhere in Premiere Elements, it is only deleted from the current project, not from your hard drive.

CREATING FOLDERS AND SUBFOLDERS IN THE MEDIA PANEL

A great way to stay organized, especially with projects where you are using lots of media, is to create folders and subfolders within the Media panel.

Start

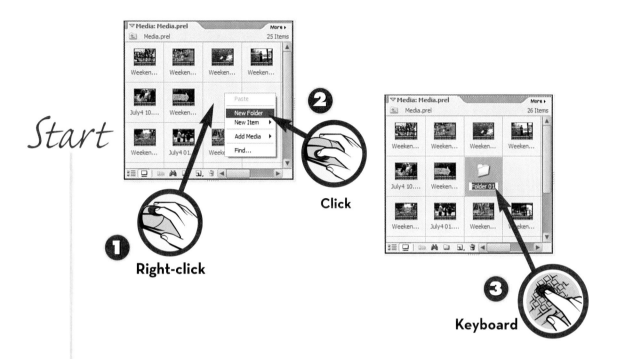

Right-click

Click

Keyboard

1 **Right-click** on an existing folder or on an empty space in the Media panel.

2 Select **New Folder** from the contextual menu.

3 A new folder is created in an available place; give the folder a new name if you don't like Premiere Elements' default one by typing over the highlighted text.

End

TIP
More on Folders
You can also create a new folder by clicking the **New Folder** button at the bottom of the Media panel. You can add media to the folder using the **Add Media** button or by dragging media already in the Media panel into the new folder.

NOTE
Getting Organized
You can create folders based on type of media (such as *Video, Music, Titles, Stills,* and so on), by subject (such as *Hannah, Davis,* or *Disneyworld*), or whatever suits your working style.

ADDING STANDARD TV MEDIA TO THE MEDIA PANEL

Premiere Elements ships with a number of standard elements that you can add to your production as needed. These include a countdown (called a Universal Counting Leader); bars with a tone (similar to what is displayed when local stations go off the air); a color matte (just a block of any color of your choice); and black video.

Start

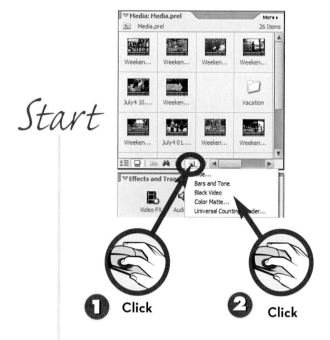

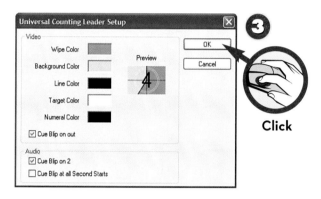

3 **Click**

1 **Click**

2 **Click**

1 Click the **New Items** button at the bottom of the Media panel, which looks a bit like a note pad.

2 Select the media you want to add from the drop-down list.

3 If you select the Universal Counting Leader, change any of the settings as needed and click **OK**.

End

NOTE

About the New Items

The Universal Counting Leader has a setup window, but Bars and Tone and Black Video have no user settings. Color Matte enables you to select the color you want for the matte from a color picker. Selecting Title opens the Title workspace.

SEARCHING FOR A MEDIA FILE

When you are working on a bigger project, one with quite a few clips, it can sometimes be a problem to find the clip you need. Scrolling through a huge list of clips and looking at the name of each clip is not very efficient. Instead, use the Premiere Elements Find function.

Start

1 Select the Media panel's **More** menu and click **Find**.

2 On the **Find** window, select the column or columns you want to search in.

3 Define your search further by choosing options from the other fields on this window, such as changing the **Operator** or the **Match** option.

4 Click **Find**.

End

NOTE

Don't Be Afraid of Boolean
You can also search on Boolean fields. That is, you can search on whether a clip has a check box checked. For example, you can search for all clips that have their Good column checked.

TIP

Quick Find, If You Don't Mind
To initiate a search, you can also click on the **Find** button at the bottom of the Media panel (the button uses a binoculars icon) or just press **Control-F**.

ASSEMBLING CLIPS ON THE TIMELINE FOR A ROUGH CUT EDIT

Although Premiere Elements doesn't have a true storyboard workspace, the Media panel can be used in that way. You can utilize the **Icon** view and the **Create Slideshow** function to create your rough cut of your video. This is a great way to get a fast first draft of your production onto the Timeline in a good sequence right away, so you can start editing, adding special effects and titles, and so on.

Click ❶

❷ Click & Drag

❶ Change the view to Icon view by clicking on the **Icon** button at the bottom of the window.

❷ Rearrange the clips as needed by dragging and dropping until they are in the desired sequence. (You can Ctrl+click to select multiple clips and drag them all at once.)

Continued

NOTE

Multimedia
Remember, media for slideshows can include not just video clips, but still images and titles, as well.

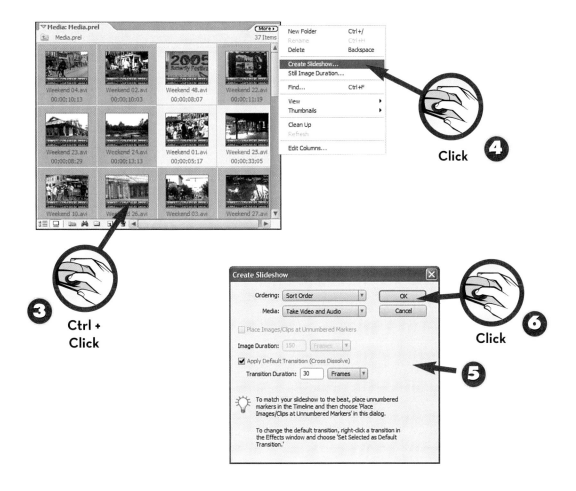

3 Select the clips you want to add to the Timeline by holding down the **Control** key and clicking on the clips, or by drawing a marquee around the clips.

4 Select **Create Slideshow** from the **More** menu or from the Premiere Elements' Project menu.

5 Select from the options on the **Create Slideshow** dialog, as needed, including the sequence order of the clips; whether to use video, audio, or both; and other factors.

6 Click **OK** to add the clips in sequence to the Timeline.

End

TIP

CTI Marks the Spot

Premiere Elements places your clips starting at the current location of the CTI on the Timeline. Move the CTI to a new location on the Timeline first if you want your clips placed at a location other than the current CTI location.

TIP

Another Access Method

You can also click the **Create Slideshow** button at the bottom of the Media panel (it looks somewhat like a stack of slides).

THE MONITOR PANEL

The Monitor panel is very similar to a television set and it's here that you play clips to see how they might work in your production; trim clips to be sure you are including only the best scenes from each clip; and play back segments of your video to see how special effects, transitions, and titles are coming along.

In fact, the Monitor panel is so much like a television set that you can even view the contents of the Monitor on a television connected to your computer through your digital camcorder. This is a great way to see how your video will ultimately look and—if you have the space on your desk—a television monitor adds a professional touch to your video-editing setup.

The Monitor panel actually operates in two distinct modes: Clip mode and Timeline mode. It looks and acts almost identical in each mode, but there are subtle differences in the interface and in how it operates. In Clip mode you can look at a source clip from the Media panel and set new start and end points for the clip. In Timeline mode you can view a clip in sequence from the Timeline and view transitions, effects, and titles. Navigation is the same no matter which mode you use.

The tasks in this part show you how to load a clip into the Monitor panel and work with it there. One of the most important skills for a video editor is to simply move about in a clip to find just the right frame. After he's there, an editor can cut, create a new start or end point (called *trimming*), zoom in or out, speed up or slow down the clip, and view effects. Knowing how to work the Monitor panel and use it to move through a clip is an essential video-editing skill that you will quickly acquire.

THE WORK-IN-PROGRESS VIEW OF YOUR WORK

The Monitor panel in Clip mode (when working with clips from the Media panel).

The Monitor panel in Timeline mode (when working with clips in sequence on the Timeline).

PLAYING A CLIP IN THE MONITOR PANEL

Use the Monitor panel to view any clip residing either in the Media panel or on the Timeline, so you can analyze the clip for its content or trim it as needed.

Double-click

①

②

Click

① To display a clip in the Monitor panel, double-click it on it either the Media panel or the Timeline panel.

② To play the clip, click the **Play** button in the Monitor panel or press the **spacebar** on your keyboard.

Continued

TIP

Play It Safe

Safe margins remind you where titles and image safely display without being clipped by the edges of the television screen. To view the safe margins, click on the Monitor panel's **More** menu in the upper-right corner and select **Safe Margins**.

3 Click

3 To pause the clip, click the **Pause** button or press the **spacebar** again.

End

TIP

Keyboard Shortcuts
Press the **L** key on your keyboard to play a clip, the **K** key to pause it, and the **J** key to play it backwards. Repeatedly pressing **J** or **L** plays the clip progressively faster (2x, 3x, and 4x).

WORKING WITH CLIPS

As you work with clips in the Monitor panel, one of the most important skills to master is moving about the clip to get to exactly the right frame.

Start

Drag

1. To move quickly through a clip, click and hold the **jog shuttle** just below the **Play** button and then slide the shuttle to the left or right to travel through the clip in either direction.

Continued

CAUTION

Need for Speed?

The faster you move the jog shuttle the faster you'll see the Current Time Indicator (CTI) bar zip by—so fast, in fact, that you'll whip from one end of a clip to another in the blink of an eye. The fix? Use the navigation bar to increase precision.

Drag

2 To see the time ruler in more detail (and thus move slower through the clip using the shuttle), drag either end of the **navigation bar** (toward the center for more precision, toward the edge to see more of the clip's time).

End

NAVIGATING A CLIP USING THE CURRENT TIMELINE INDICATOR (CTI)

The *Current Timeline Indicator (CTI)* always zips along the time ruler in the Monitor panel whenever you play a clip to show you exactly where you are in the clip. But you can also use the CTI to move around in the clip.

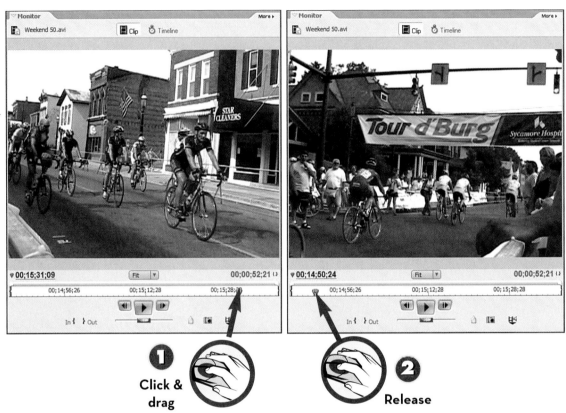

1 Click and drag the **CTI** wherever you want in the clip to view that portion of the clip.

2 The clip will move forward or backward as needed to get to the new position in the clip. (Release your mouse button to release the CTI.)

End

TIP
Timeline Travel
The CTI works the same for a clip on the Timeline. The only difference is the time ruler will be showing the length of the entire project; In other words, the CTI will be moving along the length of the whole project, not just the clip you are viewing.

TIP
Timecode Check
Notice that as you drag the CTI the time-code in the Timecode area is updating, letting you know just where the CTI is in the clip in terms of hours, minutes, seconds, and frames.

NAVIGATING A CLIP USING THE TIMECODE

The Timecode area shows you the timecode for every frame in a clip. The timecode uses the format HH;MM;SS;FF (hours; minutes; seconds; frames). If your clip shows 00;02;22;02, you're at two minutes, twenty-two seconds, frame number two. By placing your cursor here, you can drag it to move back and forth in the video clip.

Start

Click & drag left or right

Drop

1 Click directly on the numbers in the **Timecode** field and *scrub* (drag) your cursor to the left or the right to move forward and backward in the clip.

2 Release your mouse to stop scrubbing when you've reached a point in the clip you were searching for.

End

TIP

Direct Connection

If you know the timecode for a location of a clip, you can type in the exact address of that location in the Timecode field to jump directly to it. Just use the HH;MM;SS;FF format.

NOTE

Sign Language

Move ahead or back using plus and minus (+ and -) signs in the Timecode field. For example, typing **+15** moves you ahead 15 frames in the clip. You can enter up to 99 using the +/- method. (Anything more than 99 is interpreted to mean a one second jump.)

ZOOMING ON A VIDEO CLIP

The zoom feature is useful when you need to zoom in to look more closely at an image or zoom out to see the full image. Scrollbars appear when you zoom in so you can see the missing parts of the image.

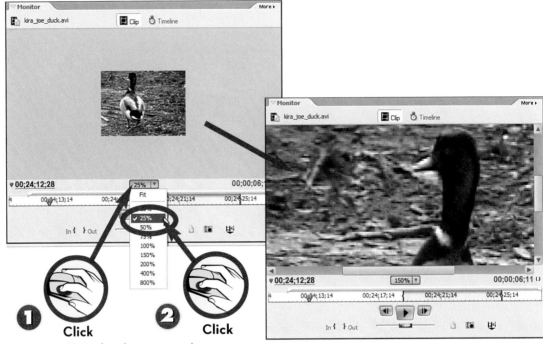

Click **Click**

Here the clip is zoomed to 25%

This is the same clip zoomed at 150% magnification.

① To zoom, click on the magnification drop-down menu, just above the Play button on the Monitor panel. By default, this menu is labeled Fit.

② Click the zoom level you need from the nine available options—from 10% all the way up to 800%.

End

Start

TIP
Magnificent Zooming
You can also use the contextual menu to zoom. Just right-click on the clip in the Monitor panel, and select **Magnification**. Then select a magnification level from the submenu.

NOTE
If the View Fits...
The **Fit** option in the Zoom menu is the default view for clips in the Monitor panel—meaning that by default Premiere Elements will first fit the clip in the Monitor panel so the entire image displays.

CHANGING THE CLIP'S START POINT

When you bring a clip into Premiere Elements, it will have a beginning and an end that are sometimes not the best start and end points for the clip. Here's how to visually select a new start point for the clip, known as *trimming in*.

Start

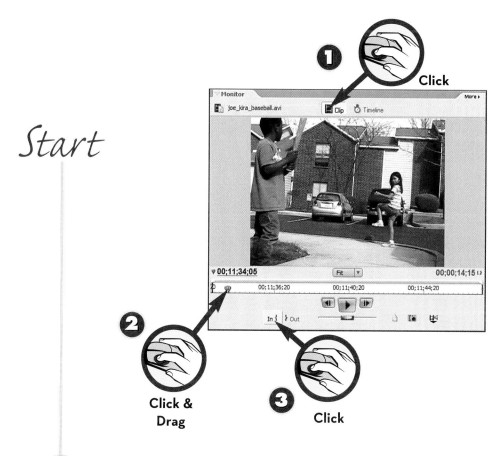

End

1. Be sure you are in Clip mode; if not, click the **Clip** button in the Monitor panel.

2. Navigate to the your new start point by clicking and dragging the **CTI**. (You can also use the jog shuttle, the **Play** button, or the Timecode field to get there.)

3. Click the **In{** button or press **I** on your keyboard.

TIP
Erasing Markers
To remove the trim-in marker, **Alt-click** the **In{** button. Or right-click on the miniature time ruler in the Monitor panel, select **Clear Clip Marker** from the menu, and then select **In**.

TIP
Split It Up
You can set the trim-in points of the audio and video tracks of a clip independently. Right-click on the time ruler in the Monitor panel and select **Set Clip Marker** from the menu, and then select either **Video In** or **Audio In**. This is known as a *split edit*.

CHANGING THE CLIP'S END POINT

An unedited clip has a beginning (called the *head*) and an end (called the *tail*). The default head and tail are often not set at the best points for the clip. This task shows you how to visually select a new end point, known as *trimming out*.

Start

Click

Click & drag

Click

1 Be sure you are in Clip mode; if not, click the **Clip** button in the Monitor panel.

2 Navigate to your new end point by clicking and dragging the **CTI** (or you can use the shuttle, the Play button, or the timecode to get there).

3 Select the **Out}** button or press **O** on your keyboard.

End

TIP

Wipe It Out

To remove the trim-out marker, Alt-click the **Out}** button. Or right-click on the miniature time ruler in the Monitor panel, select **Clear Clip Marker** from the menu, and then select **Out**.

TIP

Let's Split!

You can trim the audio and video trim-out points of a clip independently. To trim in just the video or the audio, right-click on the miniature time ruler and select **Set Clip Marker** from the menu, and then select either **Video Out** or **Audio Out**.

ADJUSTING THE CLIP'S TRIM POINTS

After you have created a start and end point for your trimmed clip, the trimmed version of the clip is represented on the Monitor panel's time ruler as a gray bar to indicate the size of the trim.

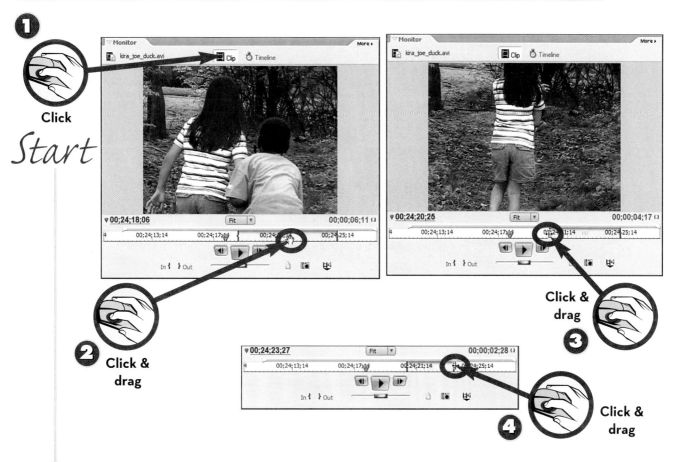

Start

Click

② Click & drag

Click & drag ③

Click & drag ④

① ** Be sure you are in Clip mode; if not, click the **Clip button in the Monitor panel.

**② ** Adjust the content in the trimmed clip by clicking the center textured area of the clip and moving the clip bar left or right. The length of the clip remains the same.

**③ ** Grab the start of the trimmed clip (the trim-in point) and drag it left or right to adjust the start of the trim. Your cursor will change to a red open bracket.

**④ ** Grab the end of the trimmed clip (the trim-out point) and drag it left or right to adjust the end of the trim. Your cursor will change to a red closed bracket.

End

TIP
Another Keyboard Shortcut
To remove all the trim markers on a clip (for in, out, video, and audio), press **G** on the keyboard.

SAVING YOUR PLACE WITH CLIP MARKERS

Clip markers act as video bookmarks, letting you quickly jump back to any marker you placed as you work on editing your movie. This task shows you how to add clip markers in the Monitor panel.

Click

Start

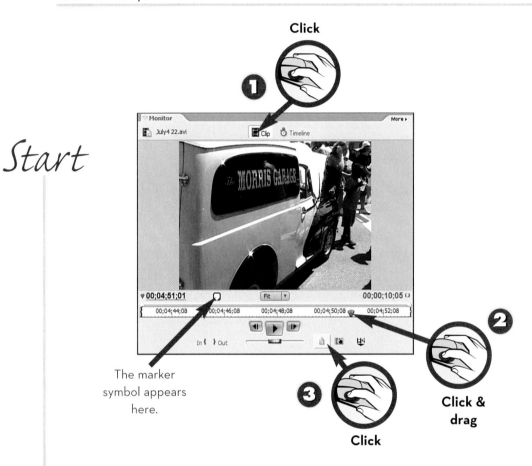

The marker symbol appears here.

Click

Click & drag

Click

1 Be sure you're in Clip mode; if not, click the **Clip** button.

2 Navigate to the frame where you want to set a marker.

3 Click the **Set Unnumbered Timeline Marker** button to add a unnumbered marker. The marker symbol appears between the Timecode and the magnification menu. The marker itself is visible on the time ruler after you move the CTI.

Continued

 TIP
Numbered or Not
You can add clip markers to any clip, either unnumbered (regular markers) or numbered markers. They work in exactly the same way; it's really just a matter of personal preference.

 TIP
Be a Star
You can also set markers using the star (multiplication) key on your numeric keypad. Press the **star key** (*) to insert a unnumbered (regular) marker; press **Shift-*** to insert a numbered marker.

Right-click

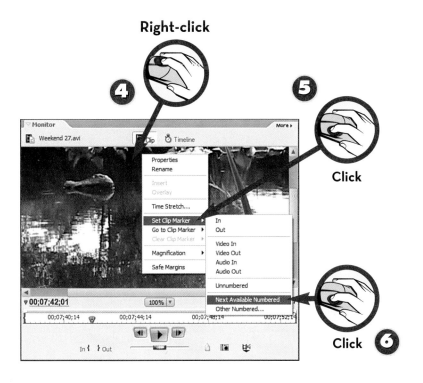

Click

Click ⑥

④ To add a numbered marker, **right-click** anywhere on the time ruler or the Monitor panel to display the contextual menu.

⑤ Select **Set Clip Marker**.

⑥ To use the next incremental number, select **Next Available Numbered**. Or to use a number of your choosing, select **Other Numbered** and enter any number up to 99.

End

NOTE

Mystery Markers

You won't see the numbers on the clip markers in the Monitor panel, but when you add the clip to the Timeline, the numbers appear clearly on each marker in the clip, allowing you to see just where you placed the markers.

TIP

A Number of Advantages

One of the advantages of using numbered markers is that you can view numbered markers in a convenient list, which also includes their timecode locations. To view the list, right-click in the time ruler and select **Go to Clip Marker**, **Numbered**.

CHANGING WHEN THE CLIP'S AUDIO STARTS OR STOPS

There may be times when you want the audio to start later or end earlier than the video for a particular clip. Premiere Elements makes that easy to accomplish.

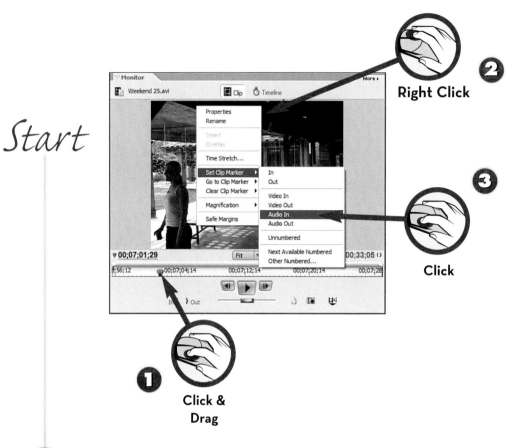

Start

Right Click

②

③

Click

①

Click & Drag

① Scrub (using the **CTI**) to the frame where you want the audio to start, or click **Play**.

② To set the audio-in point (the clip's audio track is silent up to this point), right-click the clip in the Monitor panel and select **Set Clip Marker**, **Audio In**.

Continued

TIP

Adjusting Your Adjustments

As with video trims, you can grab the audio's new trim-in and trim-out points and adjust them further. When you grab a trim point (one of the ends of the green bar in the time ruler), your cursor changes to a red bracket with a black arrow. Just drag the trim point to its new location. You can also adjust the entire audio trim by grabbing the textured area in the middle of the clip (move your mouse around the middle of the green bar until it changes to a hand) and dragging it to the left or right.

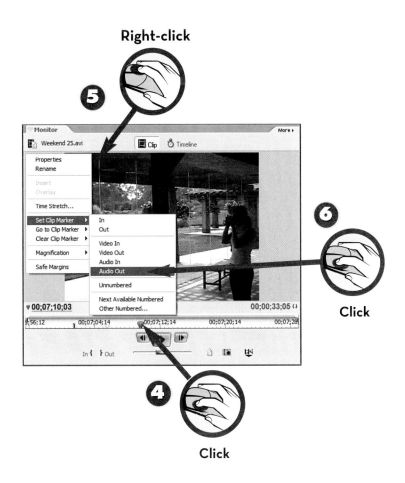

Right-click

5

6

Click

4

Click

4 Again, click **Play** or scrub (using the **CTI**) to the frame where you want the audio to stop.

5 To set the audio-out point (the clip's audio track is silent after this point), right-click the clip in the Monitor panel to access the contextual menu.

6 Select **Set Clip Marker**, **Audio Out**.

End

TIP

Seeing Green

The audio portion of the clip is a green bar on the clip's time ruler. The beginning and ending of the audio portion of the clip is then clearly different from the video portion, graphically. When you play the clip in the Monitor panel, you won't notice any difference (the audio plays as usual). But after you add the clip to the Timeline, you will see that the audio is silent outside of the area you set.

REVERSING A CLIP'S DIRECTION

With Premiere Elements, you can change the direction of a clip so it plays in reverse. Will you do great things with this ability? No, you'll do what we all do: make people jump out of the pool and back up onto the diving board, or pull food out of their mouths and put it back on their plates.

Start

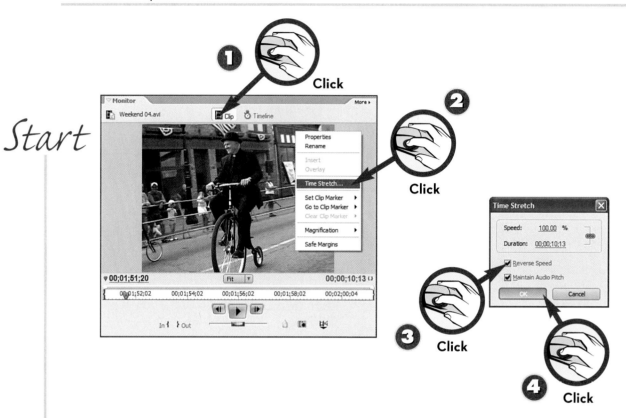

End

1 Make sure you're in Clip mode; if not, click the **Clip** button.

2 Right-click the clip in the Monitor panel to access the contextual menu and select **Time Stretch**.

3 In the Time Stretch dialog, select **Reverse Speed** to change the clip so it's running in reverse.

4 Click **OK** to reverse the clip.

TIP
Alternate Access
There are two alternate ways to get to the Time Stretch dialog. Simply use **Ctrl+R,** or select **Clip**, **Time Stretch** from the Premiere Elements menu.

NOTE
Back and Forth
To create that back-and-forth effect, such as a cat jumping a fence and then doing it again backward, first create a second copy of the clip to be the reverse version. Reverse that copy and add it to the Timeline.

CHANGING A CLIP'S SPEED (SLOW MOTION/ FAST MOTION)

You can speed up or slow down clips that you bring into the Monitor panel prior to adding them to the Timeline. The best time to change a clip's speed is before you add it to the Timeline.

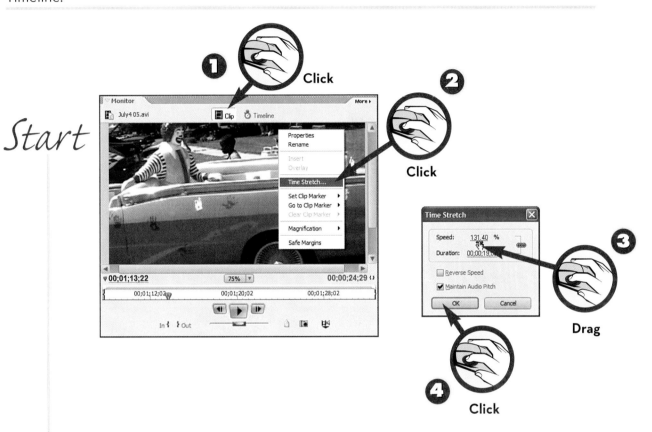

Start

Click

Click

Click

Drag

Click

End

① Make sure you're in Clip mode; if not, select the **Clip** button.

② Right-click on the clip in the Monitor panel and select **Time Stretch**.

③ In the Time Stretch dialog, scrub in the **Speed** or **Duration** time areas. Increase the number to speed up the clip; decrease it to slow it down.

④ Click **OK**.

CAUTION

Perfect Pitch

If you want the audio track to stay the same (that is, not to speed up or slow down with the action), click **Maintain Audio Pitch.**

SAVING AN IMAGE FROM A VIDEO CLIP AS A PICTURE

If there are individual frames in any video clip that you want to save as a still image, it's easy to do so in Premiere Elements. You can save a frame of video as a JPEG, GIF, TIFF, Targa, or BMP image.

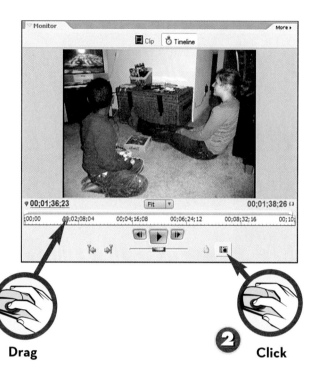

Drag

Click

1. Click and drag the **CTI** (or click the **Play** button) to navigate to the frame in the video that you want to save as a still image.

2. Click the **Export Frame** button (it looks like a camera).

Continued

TIP

Important Export

You should know of two other ways to export a frame. First, you can simply use the **Ctrl+Shift+M** keyboard shortcut as an alternative. Or, you could use the Premiere Elements menu and select **File**, **Export**, **Frame**.

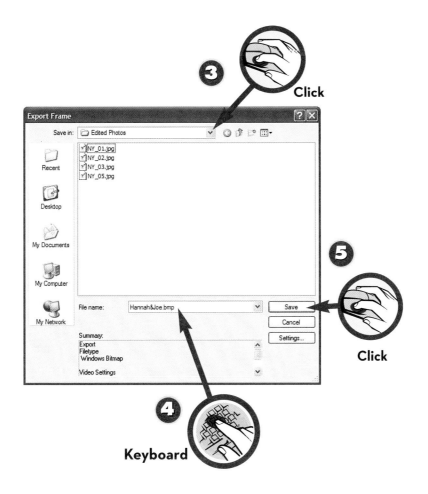

Click

Keyboard

Click

---

3 Browse to the folder where you want to save the image (or click the **New Folder** icon on the toolbar to create a new folder).

4 Type a name for the still image in the **File name** field.

5 Click **OK**.

End

TIP

Picture Perfect

Change the file format for the image by clicking the **Settings** button and choosing a different format. Premiere Elements saves still images as Windows bitmap (BMP) files by default, but you can also save as JPEG, GIF, Targa, or TIFF.

WORKING IN THE TIMELINE

The Timeline is where you assemble your movie. You drag clips from the Media panel and assemble them sequentially in the order you want your story told. In fact, clips on the Timeline are often referred to as *sequence clips*. It's here on the Timeline that your creative juices really flow, where you realize what works from clip to clip, and decide how much of a clip to use. The Timeline is where you add your special effects and titles, as well as any narration, music, or sound effects you might want to add to your final movie.

If you are creating a somewhat complicated video with multiple tracks, you might consider keeping certain types of footage on separate tracks. For example, keep photographs on one track of the Timeline, video clips on another, and titles on another. Or even organize your Timeline tracks along the lines of Highway Clips, Zoo Clips, and Birthday Clips.

The Timeline is truly the nonlinear part of Premiere Elements's nonlinear editing (NLE) system. Before computer-based video-editing systems, you had to fast-forward and rewind your way to the clips you wanted to use and assemble them onto a master video tape. Now, after you have added clips to the Media panel, you're ready to start assembling them on the Timeline—moving them around, shortening them as needed, and otherwise working on your movie as you write your video story.

THE TIMELINE IS WHERE YOU PIECE YOUR MOVIE TOGETHER

Premiere Elements's multiple video and audio tracks enable you to build your movie from smaller clips. You can be as creatively crazy or as systematically sensible as you want as you connect your clips on the Timeline until they fit together just right to tell your story.

CHANGING THE TRACK SIZE

Depending on your monitor size and resolution and your working preferences, you can customize the Timeline track size to fit your needs.

Start

End

1 To set all audio and video tracks to be one of three standard sizes, right-click on a track on the Timeline.

2 From the contextual menu, select **Track Size**.

3 Select **Small**, **Medium**, or **Large**.

TIP

Navigating the Timeline

You can move around the Timeline very quickly using your keyboard. To move to the beginning or end of your project, press **W** or **Q**. To jump to an edit point (either the start or the end of a clip), press **Pg Up** or **Pg Dn**. To move one tic in either direction, press the left or right **arrow** keys. Finally, the **Home** and **End** keys on your keyboard take you to the start (head) or end (tail), respectively, for a clip. To navigate using the mouse you drag the CTI (sometimes called the scrubber) to the left or right.

ADDING ANOTHER TRACK TO THE TIMELINE

You can add just about as many tracks to the Timeline as you need for your project. In fact, Premiere Elements allows up to 99 video (and 99 audio) tracks. This allows you to create special effects, overlay multiple effects and titles, and apply many other techniques not available if you had only a single video track.

Start

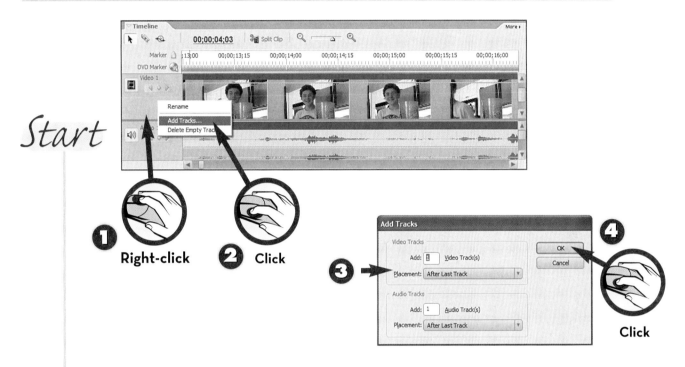

Right-click ② **Click**

Click

① Right-click on the title area of either a video track or an audio track.

② Select **Add Tracks** from the contextual menu.

③ Select the number of tracks you want to add, as well as the placement for the new tracks, in the **Add Tracks** dialog box.

④ Click **OK**.

End

TIP

Renaming a Track

Rename a track by right-clicking on the track's name (in the header area to the left) and selecting **Rename** from the contextual menu. A track name can be up to 50 characters long and the first 10 characters display by default.

TIP

Renaming a Clip

You can rename clips to help you keep track of them. To do so, right-click on the clip you want to rename and from the contextual menu select **Rename**. In the Rename Clip dialog, type the new name for the clip and click **OK**.

INSERTING OR OVERLAYING A CLIP

When you insert a clip, if room is needed for the clip on a track, video is moved aside to accommodate the new clip, thus increasing the overall length of your project. Unlike inserting a clip, overlaying a clip onto a track in the Timeline does not add to the overall length of the video.

Start

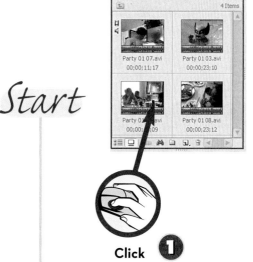

Click **1**

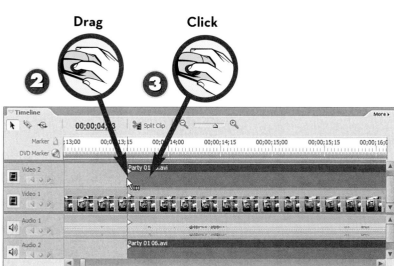

Drag   Click

1 In the Media panel, locate the clip you want to add to the Timeline.

2 Click and drag the clip to the place on the Timeline where you want the clip to appear in sequence, or hold down the **Control** key to overlay the clip.

3 Release the mouse button. (You can press the **comma** key to insert a clip or press the **period** key to overlay a clip.)

End

NOTE

Three the Short Way
To see the whole movie on the Timeline at once, press the backslash (\) key. To zoom out on the Timeline, press the minus (-) key (this doesn't work with the numeric keypad). To zoom back in, press the equal (=) key.

TIP

Zooming
Select **Timeline**, **Zoom In** to zoom in tighter on the Timeline to see a specific clip or clips, or select **Timeline**, **Zoom Out** to see more of the overall flow of your movie's story. Optionally, use the magnifying glass buttons.

SPLITTING CLIPS

One of the fundamental skills of the video editor is the effective splitting of clips into smaller pieces. By splitting clips, you have more control over what you can delete, move, and trim. Smaller clips also introduce more opportunities to add special effects, transitions, and titles and to do so with more precision.

Start

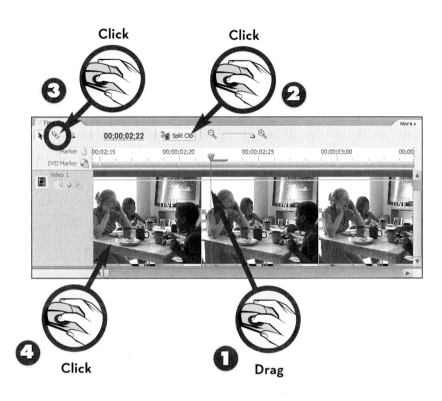

Click   **Click**

Click   **Drag**

① Drag the CTI to a location in a clip where you want to create a split.

② Click the **Split Clip** button.

③ Another way to split a clip is to click the **Razor tool** (you can also press **C** on your keyboard to activate it).

④ Using the **Razor tool**, click a point *anywhere* on a clip where you want a split.

End

TIP

Grouping Clips

It can be handy to group certain sets of clips together, so you can move them around as a unit. To do so, click on two or more clips on the Timeline. Then right-click on any of the clips and select **Group** from the contextual menu.

TIP

Don't Run with Scissors

You might expect that after you create a split, the Razor tool goes back in the drawer, but it doesn't. You might be splitting clips willy-nilly instead of clicking them. You must click on the **Selection tool** (the pointer) again.

TRIMMING CLIPS

You can shorten the duration of a clip by trimming frames from the beginning, or *head*, of the clip. This is called a *trim in*. Lengthening the clip is called a *trim out*. You can also shorten or lengthen the duration of a clip or remove unwanted footage or scenes by trimming frames from the end, also known as the tail, of the clip.

Start

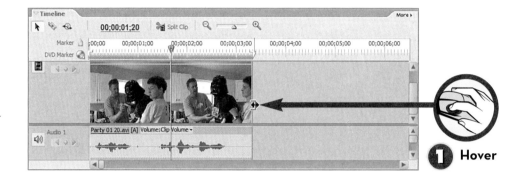

1 Hover

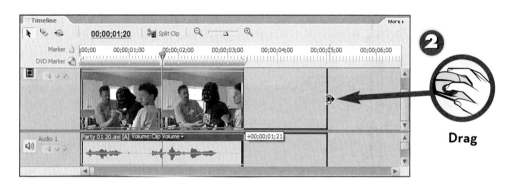

2

Drag

1 Hover the cursor at the front or back (head or tail) of a clip until you see the cursor change to the red bracket trim cursor.

2 Drag the cursor to the left or right to trim in or out, as needed.

End

TIP

A Moving Experience

As you work on your production, you can, will, and must move clips around on the Timeline tracks. When you move clips, you can choose to insert or overlay them, just as when adding clips to the Timeline. To do so, just drag the clip on the Timeline and release the mouse to drop the clip to its new location. You can move a clip from one track to another, from one location within a track to another, or even insert it right in the middle of another clip.

SPEEDING UP OR SLOWING DOWN A CLIP

Because altering the speed of a clip is such a regular part of what a video editor does, Premiere Elements provides a tool right on the Timeline for doing this.

Click

Start

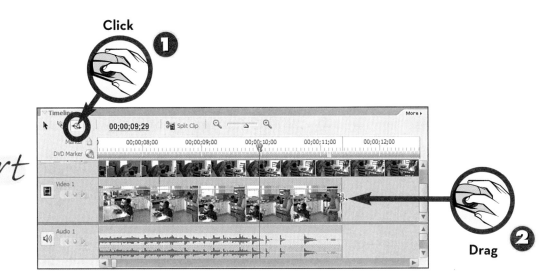

Drag

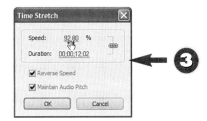

1 Click the **Time Stretch tool** (or press **X** on your keyboard to activate it).

2 Select the head or the tail (front or back) of any clip. Drag the clip tighter to make it speed up or drag it wider to make it slow down.

3 For more precision, use the Time Stretch dialog box by pressing **Ctrl+R** (select the clip first) or by right-clicking on any clip and selecting **Time Stretch**.

End

TIP

Open a Dialog

In the Time Stretch dialog, you can precisely enter the speed, duration, and whether to maintain the audio pitch (that is, whether to speed that up or slow it down, too). You can return a clip to normal speed by setting the **Speed** to 100%. By the way, another regular trick in the arsenal of any good video editor is reversing a clip. The reverse function is found on the Time Stretch dialog, as well. To activate it, select the **Reverse Speed** check box.

ADDING TIMELINE MARKERS

Timeline Markers are useful as bookmarks for marking clips or scenes within clips that contain important information or pivotal moments in your video. By creating Timeline Markers (and optionally naming them using a description), you don't have to remember exactly where a scene is.

Click

Drag

Start

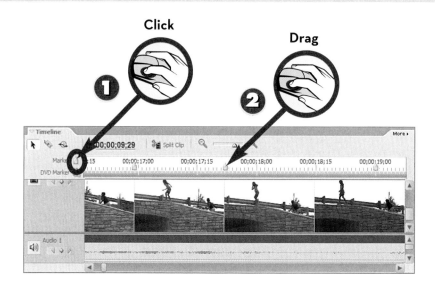

① Select the **Marker icon** and drag it across the time ruler to the point in your video where you want to add a new *unnumbered* Timeline Marker.

② Release the mouse to insert the Marker.

End

 TIP
Mark This Way
You can also move the CTI where you want to add a marker and right-click on the time ruler and select **Set Timeline Marker, Unnumbered** from the contextual menu.

 TIP
Not Just Another Number
You can set numbered Timeline Markers by selecting **Set Timeline Marker, Next Available Numbered** or **Set Timeline Marker, Other Numbered**. This places markers on the time ruler with little numbers in them.

ADDING DVD MARKERS

Premiere Elements can automatically build the DVD chapters and associated menu buttons for your movie based on the DVD Markers you place. Just place DVD Markers at the beginning of any clip you want to be a DVD chapter and Premiere Elements does the rest.

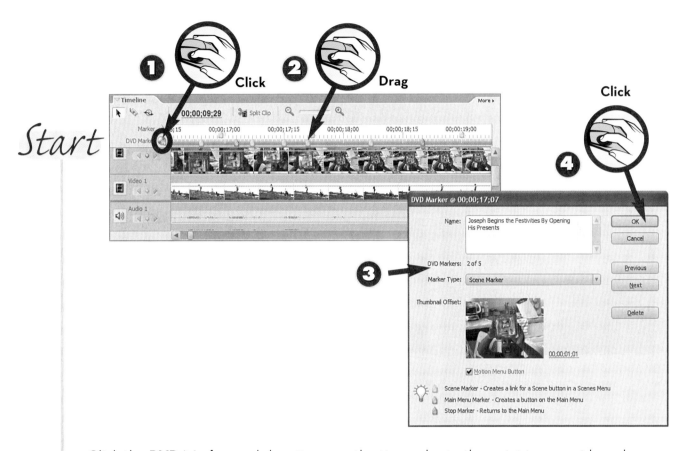

Start

Click **Drag** **Click**

End

1 Click the **DVD Marker** and drag it across the time ruler to the point in your video where you want a new DVD chapter to begin.

2 Release the mouse to insert the DVD Marker. The marker is placed.

3 The DVD Marker window displays. Here, you can enter a name for the DVD Marker, select a marker type, choose a thumbnail image in the DVD Marker window, and more.

4 Click **OK** when you're done to close the DVD Marker window.

TIP

So Many Ways...

To have Premiere Elements set DVD markers for you, choose **Marker**, **Auto-Generate DVD Markers**. Then choose your settings from the Automatically Set DVD Scene Markers dialog box and click **OK**. You can also right-click the time ruler where you want a DVD chapter to start and select **Set DVD Marker**.

NOTE

So Many Types...

You can set any of the three types of DVD markers as you work: a Scene Marker (green), a Main Menu Marker (blue), and a Stop Marker (red).

WORKING WITH TRANSITIONS

The first thing you should understand about transitions is that you should *avoid* using them! That's right. Although transitions have their place, they almost always call attention to themselves and anything that calls attention away from the story can potentially ruin the experience for your viewers. You should always be in control of your story and your art (which, in this case, is video editing), so be in control, too, of how and when you use transitions.

You will find that there will be times when you want to call attention to a change in your story, such as a change of location or to show the passage of time. A transition such as a fade to black or a slow dissolve might work perfectly in such cases. In other cases, transitions can add to the fun. For example, if you are making a comedy video you can actually use transitions for a comic effect (think funniest home videos). Or, you might be making a genealogy video that includes pictures of your ancestors and you want to use transitions more in sync with the rest of the old-time feel of your project. These are just a couple of good reasons to use transitions. George Lucas intentionally used transitions and wipes in his *Star Wars* movies for that movie serial look that he remembered watching growing up.

But the video editor's best friend is the basic cut; just moving directly from one scene to another, and from that one to the next, without any transition at all. Try it and you'll see that most of the time it works perfectly! Occasionally you might want to fade out from one scene (most typically to black) and fade up to the next scene (again, usually from black). All that said, you should have fun making your videos, so if you want to throw in every transition Premiere Elements offers, plus the kitchen sink, by all means do so.

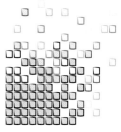

PREMIERE ELEMENTS OFFERS A RICH SELECTION OF TRANSITIONS

Premiere Elements includes more than 75 transitions. There are 10 3D Motion transitions, 7 Iris transitions, 5 Page Peels, 12 Slides, 6 Special Effects transitions, 5 Stretch transitions, 17 Wipes, 6 Dissolves, 4 Zooms, and 5 GPU (graphics processing unit–dependent) transitions.

Choose from 3D Motion transitions...

...to Page Peel transitions...

...to Dissolves, and everything in between.

ADDING A TRANSITION TO A CLIP OR BETWEEN TWO CLIPS

Adding a transition between two clips in Premiere Elements is very simple. Just choose the transition you want to use from the Effects and Transitions panel and drag and drop it on the Timeline.

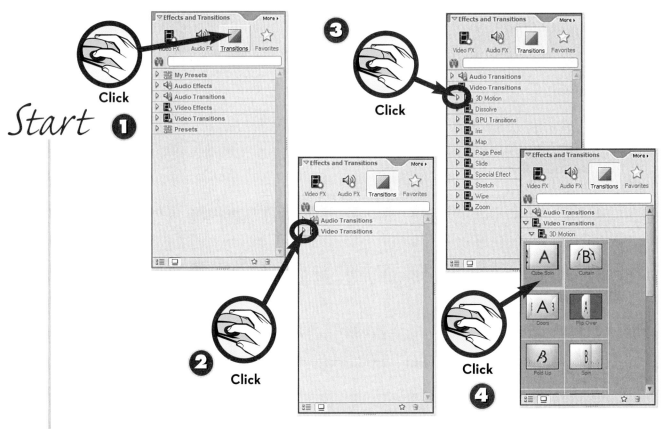

Start

1 On the Effects and Transitions panel, click the **Transitions** button.

2 Click the **arrow** next to the Video Transitions folder to open it.

3 Click on the **arrow** next to any of the video transitions category folders to view the transitions available for that category.

4 Click on an effect to see an animation of how the effect works.

Continued

TIP

Beginning, Middle, and End

The mouse cursor changes to show you whether the transition is applied to the beginning or end of a single clip, or between two clips. The cursor looks like a flag with the wind blowing from the west when it is a transition for the beginning of a clip, like a flag in an easterly wind for an end-of-clip transition, and something like a spindle for a between-clips transition.

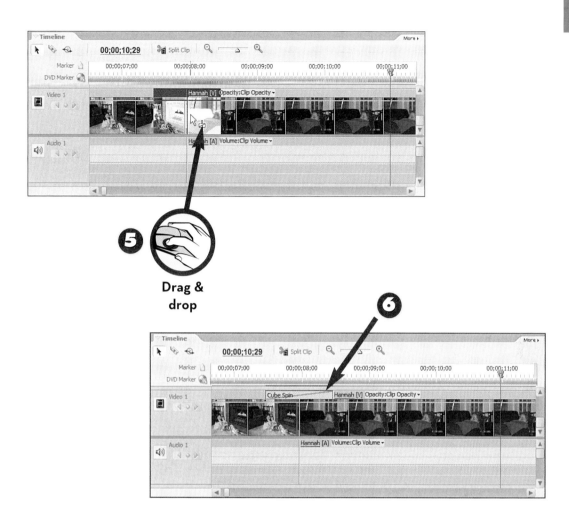

Drag & drop

5 Drag the transition you want to use to the Timeline and drop it between two clips or onto a single clip.

6 Notice how transitions appear on the timeline as purple boxes with a single diagonal line across the middle.

End

PREVIEWING HOW A TRANSITION WILL LOOK

You can preview how a transition operates and how it will look using the Properties panel. The Properties panel enables you to tweak the settings for a transition, as well.

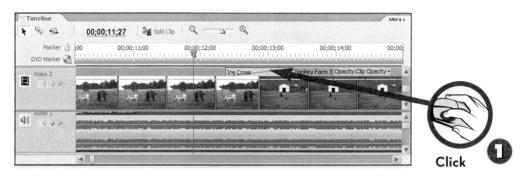

Click **1**

Start

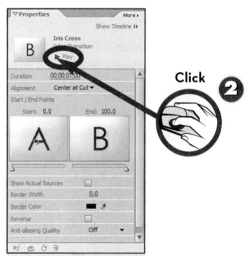

Click **2**

1 To view the properties for a transition, click on the purple **transition area** of a clip on the Timeline.

2 Click on the miniature **Play** button toward the top of the Properties panel to see how the transition works. (Once clicked, the Play button turns into the Stop button.)

Continued

TIP

Living Large

If you want to see the transition at a larger view than this miniature version, use the Monitor panel. Position the CTI a bit before the transition on the Timeline (and be sure the Monitor panel is set to show the Timeline, not a clip). Press the **Play** button on the Monitor panel and watch the transition there and see approximately how the transition will look.

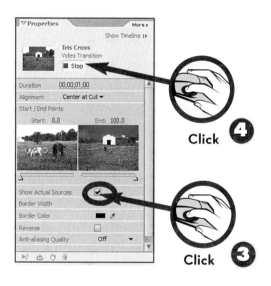

Click 4

Click 3

3 To view the transition using the actual clips, click the **Show Actual Sources** check box.

4 Click the **Stop** button (where the Play button used to be) to stop the transition from playing (otherwise, it continues looping).

End

RENDERING A TRANSITION

To *render* in video-editing terms simply means to apply something, such as a special effect, title, or transition. Until you render, what you are looking at is Premiere Elements's approximation of what the transition will look like. After it is rendered, the transition is much smoother and runs faster.

Start

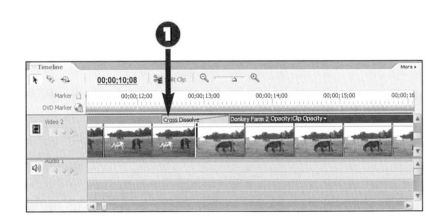

1 Clips that have effects or transitions associated with them are identified in Premiere Elements by a red bar above them. (Clips that have had effects rendered have a green bar.)

Continued

NOTE

Lots of Rendering, No Waiting!

Although Premiere Elements has one of the fastest rendering engines available, it can still take quite some time to render a long movie with many effects, transitions, and titles. One way to avoid long waits is to render after you're satisfied with each transition you've created. You can always change it later.

Click

If at any time you want to render all transitions, effects, and titles you've added to your project, press the **Enter** key on your keyboard. You'll see the Rendering dialog box pop up to keep you informed of the progress, including the number of frames rendered out of the total and the estimated time remaining.

If you want to render later, click **Cancel**. You can also let the rendering progress until the red bar above the clip you want to render has turned green and then click Cancel. You'll still need to render the other clips later.

End

TIP

Remember, Press Enter to Render

In keeping with the previous note, get in the habit of pressing the **Enter** key after you've finished working with a transition (or a title or special effect, for that matter) to apply it. By doing so, you'll be rendering as you go.

MODIFYING A TRANSITION

All of Premiere Elements's transitions work perfectly out of the box; they all are set to work within a one-second timeframe, for example. In the case of transitions positioned between clips, the transitions are set to work 50% on one clip and 50% on the other by default. You can modify transitions to work the way *you* want.

Start

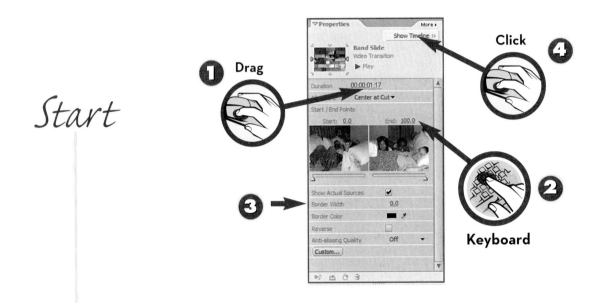

1 Change the duration for any transition by dragging a new duration in the timecode area for the transition in the Properties panel.

2 To change the transition's start and end times, enter a new time above the A/B preview areas in either the **Start** or **End** field.

3 If available, adjust border color and width, anti-aliasing quality (image smoothing), and other settings.

4 Click **Show Timeline** to open the Timeline view to change the duration of the transition and other factors.

Continued

TIP

Alignment Assignment

You also have the option of setting when the transition begins: at the beginning of a clip, at the end of a clip, between two clips, or a custom setting by selecting from the **Alignment** drop-down menu.

TIP

Who's Default Is It?

You can select any transition you want to be the default used with the Create Slideshow function. Right-click on a transition in the Effects and Transitions panel. Click **Set Selected As Default Transition**.

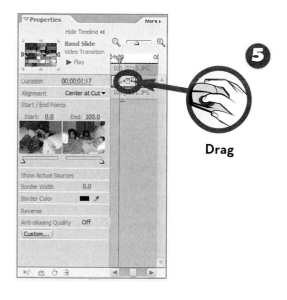

Drag

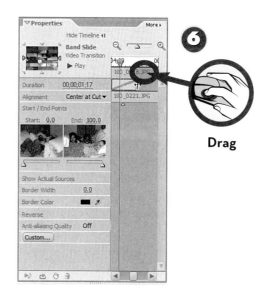

Drag

5 When the cursor looks like a black box with a bidirectional arrow through it, you can move the transition left or right while simultaneously changing the percentage of the transition for each clip.

6 When the cursor looks like a red bracket with a black arrow through it you can adjust the length of the transition, either from the head or tail end.

End

CREATING THE CLASSIC FADE TO BLACK TRANSITION

The best writing uses few if any adjectives and adverbs. Pick up any classic literature and see. The best movies use few if any transitions. Watch any classic movie and see. But you will see one transition used, other than the pure and simple cut, and that is the fade to black/fade up from black. It's as classic as the cut, and just as effective.

Start

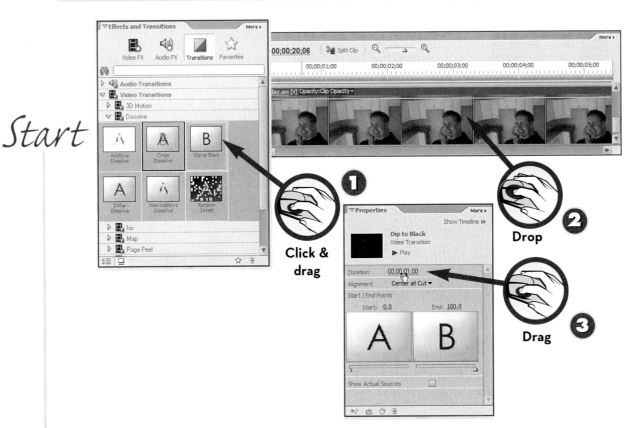

Click & drag

Drop

Drag

1 From the Dissolve transitions category, select **Dip to Black** (*dip* is Premiere Elements's word for *fade* here).

2 Drag and drop it to the clip or clips in the **Timeline** that you want to have fade down to or up from black.

3 In the **Properties panel**, modify the duration of the fade as desired by dragging in the number field.

End

NOTE

It's the End of the Movie As We Know It

Although you can fade to black and fade up from black in the middle of your movie, the effect is most typically used at the beginning and end of a film, to signify "we are about to begin" and "the movie has ended..."

TIP

My Little Black Box

If you want extra blackness for this transition, drop a black video clip from the Media panel where needed. Black video is available from the **New Media** button (it looks like a notepad, next to the garbage can) on the Media panel.

CREATING A DISSOLVE

Of all the transition types, the dissolve is the subtlest. It is the Zen of transitions, having a calming effect on the audience. Alright, if not a calming effect, it is the least intrusive. The fade to black discussed in the preceding task is in the dissolve family.

Start

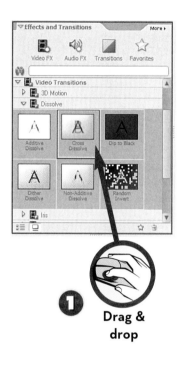

①
Drag & drop

① Select one of the transitions from the **Dissolve** category and drag and drop it onto your clip or clips on the Timeline.

② Modify the settings for the transition in the **Properties panel** if desired.

End

NOTE

Plop, Plop; Fizz, Fizz

There are six Dissolves available in Premiere Elements: the Additive Dissolve, the non-Additive Dissolve, the Cross Dissolve, the Dither Dissolve, the Random Invert, and the Dip to Black.

CREATING A WIPE

After the Dissolve, the Wipe is the next most common type of transition. With the Wipe, however, you now enter into the "hey, look at me!" realm of transitions. Granted, the Wipe is at the less intrusive end of the scale, but don't be fooled. Everyone in your audience is now thinking: "Hey, look! A wipe!" and they are no longer thinking about the story, if only for duration of the Wipe.

Start

Drag & drop

① Select one of the transitions from the **Wipe** category and drag and drop it onto your clip or clips on the Timeline.

② You can modify the settings for the transition in the **Properties panel** if desired. Some Wipes have more elaborate controls than others—experiment with them until you get just the look you want.

End

NOTE

Clean Wipes

There are 17 Wipes available in Premiere Elements: Band Wipe, Barn Doors, Checkerboard, Clock Wipe, Gradient Wipe, Inset, Paint Splatter, Pinwheel, Radial Wipe, Random Blocks, Random Wipe, Spiral Boxes, Venetian Blinds, Wedge Wipe, Wipe, and finally, Zig-Zag Blocks.

CREATING AN IRIS-STYLE TRANSITION

After the Dissolve and the Wipe, the next most common and perhaps next least intrusive transitions are in the Iris category. The Iris transitions simulate the look of a camera lens opening.

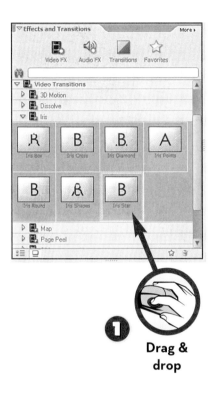

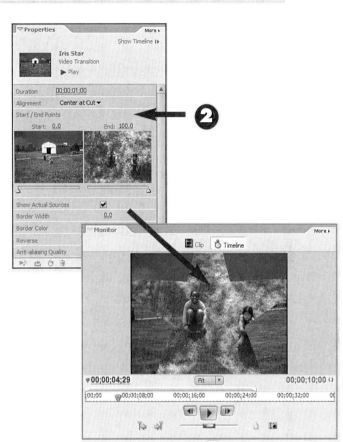

Drag & drop

Start

End

1 Select one of the transitions from the **Iris** category and drag and drop it onto your clip or clips on the Timeline.

2 You can modify the settings for the transition in the **Properties panel**, if desired.

CREATING A PAGE-PEEL TRANSITION

Page Peel transitions can be a lot of fun. As the name implies, the transition creates the illusion of a page being turned. The current scene is on the page being turned away, and the new scene is on the page at which your audience is now looking. This is a nice set of transitions for a "this is your life" type of video.

Start

1 **Drag & drop**

2

1 Select one of the transitions from the **Page Peel** category and drag and drop it onto your clip or clips on the Timeline.

2 You can modify the settings for the transition in the **Properties panel**, if desired.

End

CREATING SLIDE AND STRETCH TRANSITIONS

Slide transitions give the illusion of one clip sliding out or being pushed out of view while a new clip comes into view. Stretch transitions give the illusion of the clip being distorted or stretched in some way as the outgoing clip is moved out of the way of the incoming clip.

Start

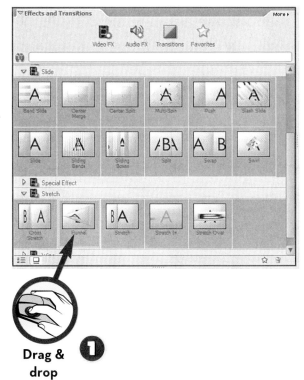

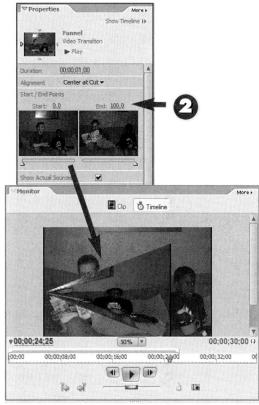

Drag & drop

①

① Select one of the transitions from the **Slide** or **Stretch** categories and drag and drop it onto your clip or clips on the Timeline.

② Modify the settings for the transition in the **Properties panel**, if desired.

End

NOTE

Whose Slide Are You On?

There are 12 Slide transitions in Premiere Elements: Band Slide, Center Merge, Center Split, Multi-Spin, Push, Slash Slide, Slide, Sliding Bands, Sliding Boxes, Split, Swap, and Swirl!

NOTE

That's Quite a Stretch

In addition, there are five Stretch transitions in Premiere Elements: Cross Stretch, Funnel, Stretch, Stretch In, and Stretch Over.

CREATING A ZOOM TRANSITION

With Zoom transitions, the clips appear to zoom in or out as one clip exits and another enters.

Start

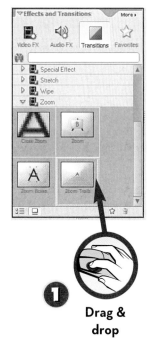

Drag & drop

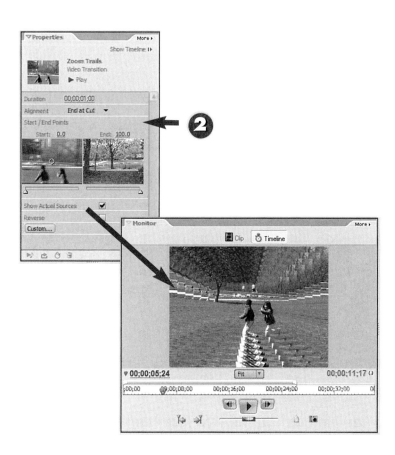

① Select one of the transitions from the **Zoom** category and drag and drop it onto your clip or clips on the Timeline.

② You can modify the settings for the transition in the **Properties panel**, if desired.

End

NOTE

Zoom with a View

There are four Zoom transitions available in Premiere Elements, each of which has a different and quite interesting look. Aside from the basic Zoom transition, you also have the Cross Zoom , Zoom Boxes, and Zoom Trails.

TIP

Knowing the Customs

Two of the Zoom transitions have Custom buttons that enable you to further customize the transition. Use it on Zoom Boxes to modify the number of boxes and their size. Use it on Zoom Trails to modify the number of trails.

CREATING A 3D MOTION TRANSITION

3D Motion transitions are very animated and entertaining transitions that make a statement on their own, almost as much as the contents of the clip itself. If you fold up a clip or have it tumble away, in a sense you could be making a commentary on the contents of the clip. These transitions are best when used for funny videos.

Start

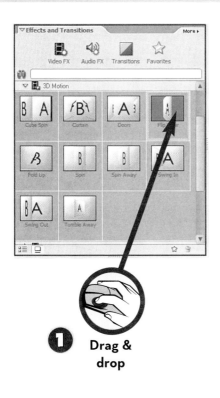

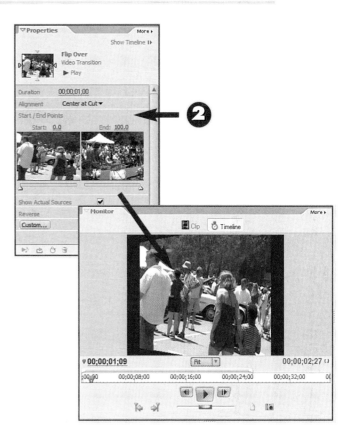

1 Drag & drop

1 Select one of the transitions from the **3D Motion** category and drag and drop it onto your clip or clips on the Timeline.

2 You can also modify the settings for the transition in the **Properties panel**, if desired.

End

CREATING A SPECIAL EFFECT TRANSITION

Special Effect transitions allow you to create a transition to move from one scene to the next that uses changes in color and other special effects, as opposed to normal effects that use motion or the illusion of motion, such as a page peeling away. These are transitions for special purposes only and you might find you rarely, if ever, find a purpose for them in your projects.

Start

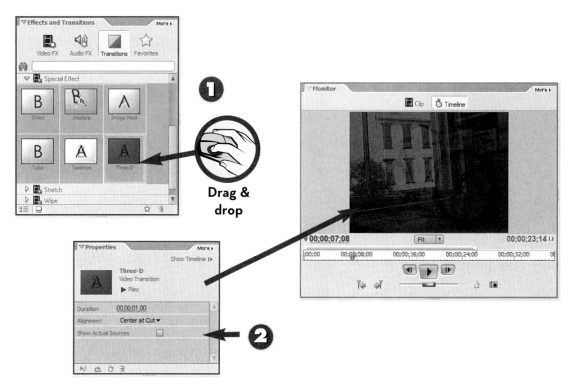

Drag & drop

 Select one of the transitions from the **Special Effect** category and drag and drop it onto your clip or clips on the Timeline.

Q You can also modify the settings for the transition in the **Properties panel**, if desired.

End

NOTE

Extra Special Effects

There isn't just one Special Effect transition with Premiere Elements, but six. You can choose from Direct, Displace, Image Mask, Take, Texturize, and Three-D when you feel the need for a Special Effect type of transition. Note that there is, on occasion, a Custom button here for some of these transitions to enable you to further customize how the transition works.

ADDING A COLOR BORDER TO A TRANSITION

A number of transitions, where one clip moves in and the preceding clip moves out, have edges of clips on screen at the same time. You might want to add a line of color to that edge.

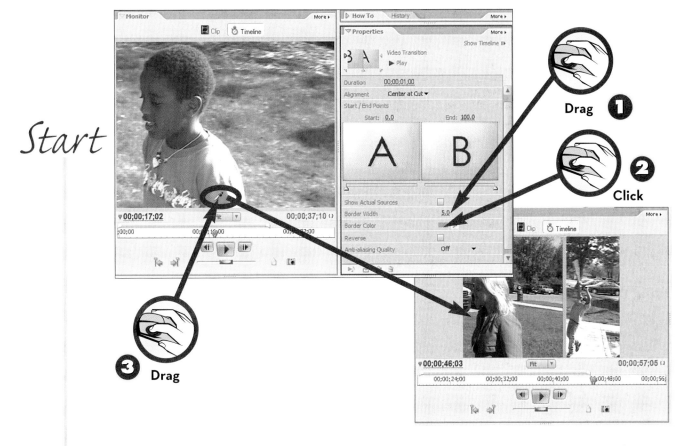

Start

Drag ❶

Click ❷

Drag ❸

End

❶ After applying the transition, drag the **Border Width** setting in the Properties panel to something other than zero (up to 100.0).

❷ Click on the **black box** in the Border Color field to select a different color from the color picker.

❸ To use a color from a media clip (or from anywhere else on the screen), drag the **eyedropper** around the screen and release when you find the color you want.

TIP
What Color Is That?
As you pass over colors on the screen with the eyedropper, the color directly underneath the eyedropper displays in the Border Color color block. When you see the color you want in the color block, simply release your mouse.

NOTE
Trouble at the Border
Unless you set the Border Width greater than zero, you won't see the border display. You'll know you got it right because your border displays in the right color and in relative thickness in the Preview window after you click **Play**.

ADDING TITLES AND TEXT TO YOUR MOVIES

Imagine having to explain to your viewers every time that the guy talking in your video right now is the owner of this great restaurant you ate at on vacation, or that this woman is the artist who created that statue downtown that you filmed as part of this video. That might be fun the first time, but it would get tiring quickly. Moreover, you can't always be there to explain who is who. So, what's a filmmaker to do? It's easy—just label people and things just like they do in professional documentaries and television shows. This is accomplished through titles.

Titles—and text on the screen in general—are a vital part of your video. Without titles, you won't really have a finished video with a professional look. Titles in Premiere Elements enable you to add opening and closing credits; to identify characters (your family and friends), locations, and dates; and label new scenes.

As for titles, every movie should have a name, even if it's just "Our Vacation" or "Joe's Birthday." You should give yourself credit, too, as in "A Film by Eugene Scorsese," "Edited by E. Scorsese," or "From a Concept by E. Scorsese." Hey, why be shy? End credits enable you to scroll or roll more detailed credits about the music you used, the locations you shot in, the people who helped you—even your dog. It's your film: Thank whoever you want!

TITLES MAKE YOUR MOVIE COME ALIVE

You can create amazingly crazy or subtly simple titles with Premiere Elements to exactly match your personality and the subject or mood of your movie.

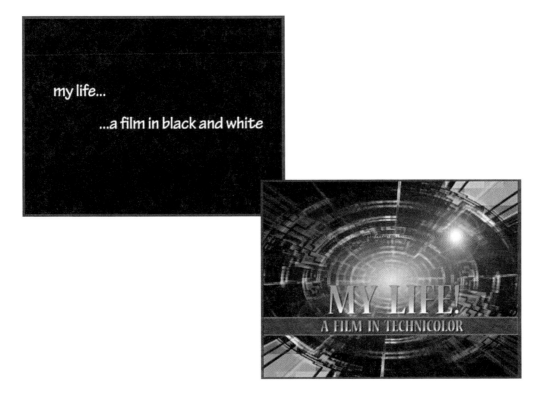

SELECTING A TITLE TEMPLATE

Premiere Elements includes dozens of templates to get you started. Each template can be modified as much or as little as you need. Premiere Elements includes templates for weddings, birthdays, graduations, vacations, and more.

Start

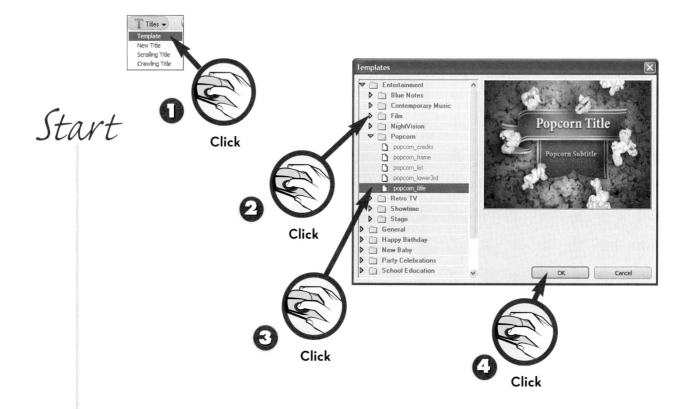

Click

Click

Click

Click

1 Click and hold the Titles button and select **Template**.

2 Click the arrow next to any of the template themes to view what's available.

3 Select a template type (such as main title, frame, lower third, and so on).

4 Click **OK** and the title appears in the Titler, ready for you to start customizing.

End

TIP
Change Is Good
You can modify anything and everything on the template with which you start. You'll want to change the placeholder text. But you can also change the font, the font color, the text location, and the graphics.

TIP
Safety First
To turn on the safe text guidelines, select **More**, **Safe Title Margin** so you won't end up with a letter or two cut off when you watch the DVD on a TV screen. For the video itself, select **Safe Action Margin**.

STARTING WITHOUT A TEMPLATE

You can create a title starting with a blank slate, if needed, and select fonts, objects, and other elements to create a custom title.

Click

1

Start

Keyboard

2

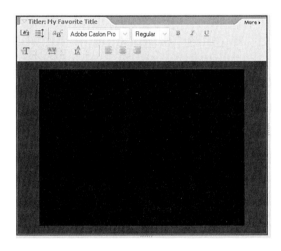

3

Click

1 Click and hold on the Titles button and select **New Title**.

2 Type a name for the template in the **New Title** dialog (or use the default name supplied by Premiere Elements).

3 Click **OK** and the Titler opens black and without a template in it.

End

TIP

A Pop-Cornucopia of Templates

Before you start creating a title from scratch, look through Premiere Elements's templates to see if there's one there that fits the bill. You can always make changes if there's one that's close but not quite right.

TIP

Back in Black

If you want to concentrate on what you're doing without distraction, you can keep the video areas of the Titler black. But to get a real sense of how your titles and text are going to look with your videos, click **Show Video** on the Titler's **More** menu.

ADDING TEXT

If you are starting from scratch, you can enter text anywhere on the Titler. If you are using a template, just select the existing placeholder text and start typing.

Start

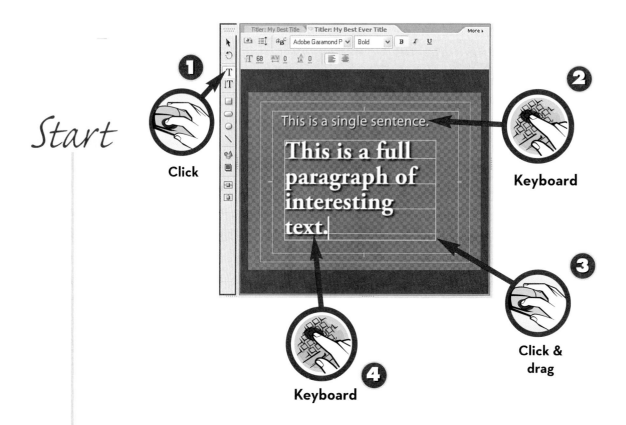

Click

Keyboard

Keyboard

Click & drag

1 In the Titler, click the **Type** tool (it's the button that looks like a capital *T*).

2 To create poster or title text, click anywhere and start typing (you can also select any existing text and type over it).

3 To create a paragraph's worth of text (or more), click and drag on the page to create a text box.

4 Start typing in the box.

End

 TIP
Default Line
When you start typing, whatever style is selected in the Styles palette and whatever type size is currently set will be the style and size of your text. Of course, any text attribute can be changed at any time.

 TIP
Not Written in Stone
You might find that after you have entered your title, it's not at all where you want it to be. To move it, click on the **Selection Tool** (the arrow button), and click and drag the text block to wherever you want.

ENTERING VERTICAL TEXT

Premiere Elements has a special tool, the Vertical Type tool, for entering vertical text. Vertical text is basically stacked text, where one letter stacks on top of the next and the letters are upright. This is different from text rotated 90°, where the letters appear on their side.

Start

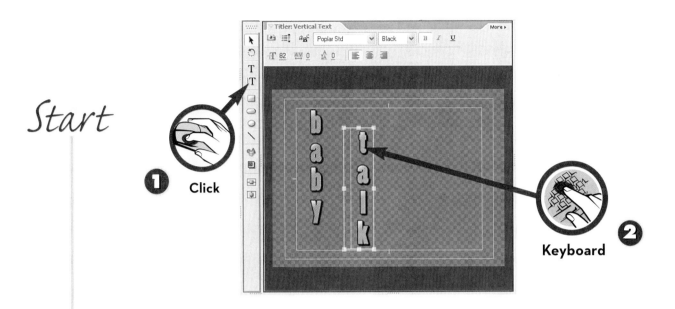

1 Click

2 Keyboard

1 In the Titler, click the **Vertical Type tool** (it looks like a capital *T* with a down arrow next to it).

2 For a single word, just type your text. (For a paragraph of vertical text, drag a text box first.)

End

NOTE

Acronym Names

Vertical text can be a fun way to introduce an acronym. Type the acronym using vertical text and then define the acronym using horizontal text.

TIP

Cool Vertical Runnings

If you want to have text running vertically and not just stack one letter on top of another, you can rotate any text so that it's sideways (like the spine of a book). For information on how to do this, see the "Rotating Text" task.

ROTATING TEXT

Besides having text run horizontally across the screen (left to right) or vertically (top to bottom) you can *skew*, or rotate, text so that it runs at an angle.

Start

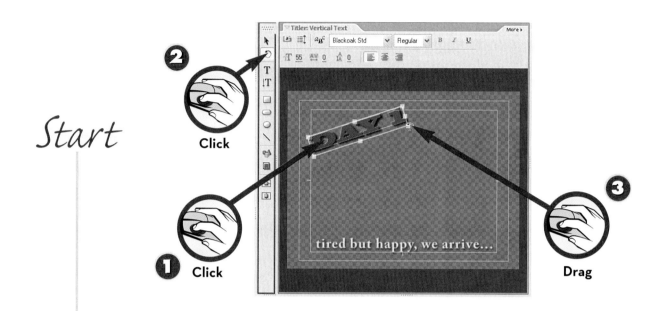

2 Click

1 Click

3 Drag

1 Select the text you want to skew.

2 Select the **Rotation tool**.

3 Click anywhere on the text and drag in any direction until you decide it looks right.

End

TIP
Dark Shadows
If the text you rotated had a drop shadow, the drop shadow might look a little funny at the top of the letters. To move the shadow back to a logical shadowy location, select the **Color Properties** button and then adjust the shadow.

TIP
Precision Rotation
To rotate a block of text to an exact amount, **right-click** on the text and select **Transform**, **Rotation**. Enter the rotation degree (from 1 to 359.99) in the **Rotation** dialog. If you enter 90, the text will rotate to true 90°, starting at zero.

CHOOSING A TYPE STYLE

If you are using a template, the font, font color, and other type settings have already been selected for you. You can change these as a group by selecting a different style.

Start

Click

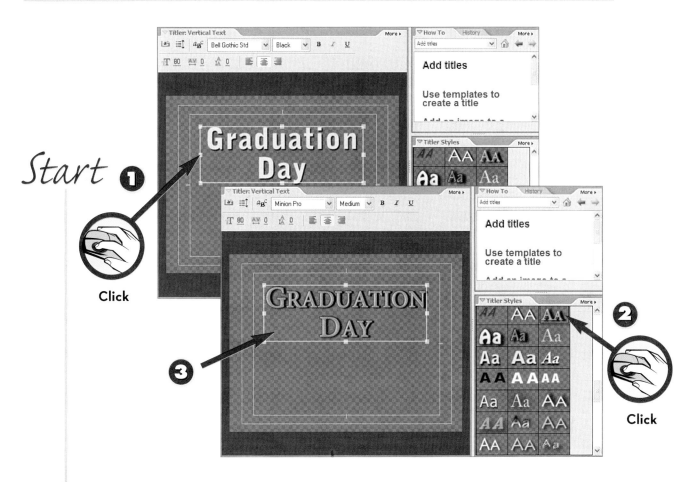

Click

1. Select the text you want to change by clicking on it.

2. Click one of the available Premiere Elements **Styles** on the right side of the dialog box to change the text to that style.

3. The text changes to the new style including font, color, and whatever other attributes that style includes.

End

MANUALLY CHOOSING A FONT

You can manually choose any font you want for any paragraph, sentence, word, or even single letter in a title. You can use the Fonts drop-down menu or the Fonts browser to make your choice.

Start

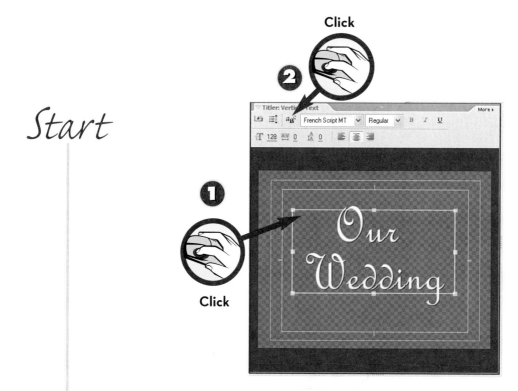

Click

Click

① Select the text you want to change by clicking on it.

② Select the **Font Browser** button.

Continued

TIP

Easy Shopping

Because the font changes you make appear on the screen instantly, you can click, observe the change, and click on another font until you find the perfect one. You can also view fonts by selecting a font from the **Fonts** drop-down menu or by **right-clicking** on the text and selecting **Font** from the contextual menu.

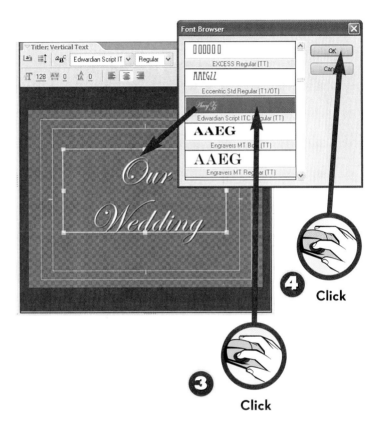

3 Click

4 Click

3 Click on fonts in the Font Browser to see them applied to the selected text.

4 When you've decided on a font, click **OK**.

End

CHANGING THE COLOR OF TEXT OR AN OBJECT

You can change the color of text (or an object) using the Color Properties dialog box. The Color Properties dialog box also gives you the ability to apply a gradient effect or add a drop shadow.

Start

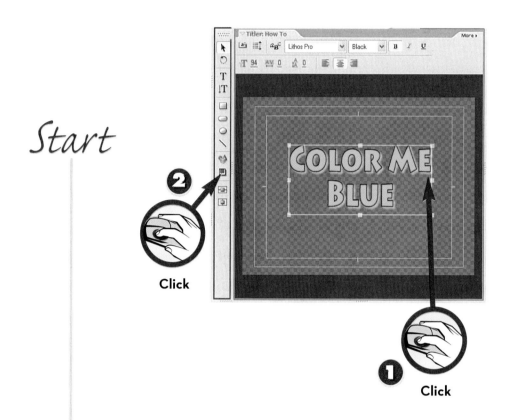

Click

Click

1 In the **Titler**, select the text or object whose color you want to change.

2 Select the **Color Properties** button.

Continued

TIP
Color Coded
You can enter RGB numeric values for a color instead of clicking on a color if you are trying to match a color's specific RGB values. Or if there is a cool color already on the screen (in a video image on the Timeline, for example), use the Eyedropper tool to select it!

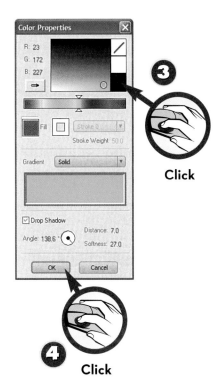

Click

Click

③ Select a color from the color swatch on the Color Properties window, and optionally select a **Gradient** type and the **Fill** and **Stroke** (the letter's outline).

④ Click **OK**.

End

CHANGING TEXT SIZE

Premiere Elements supports almost infinite adjustments in font size, so you can make the text appear on screen exactly the way you want. You can accomplish this several ways, as noted in the following steps.

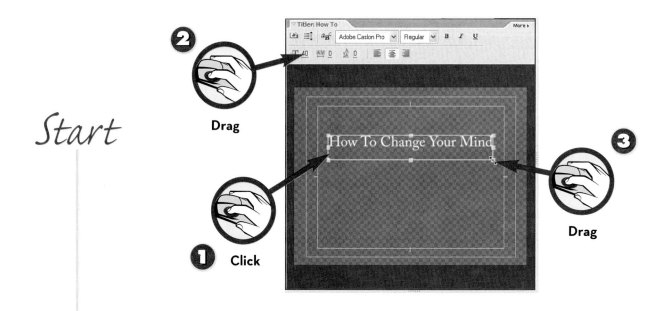

Start

Drag

Click

Drag

1 In the Titler, select the text you want to change.

2 You can change the type size by dragging the mouse cursor left or right across the Type Size field or by typing a new size in this field.

3 You can also change the type size by dragging the bottom or corner selection points of the text box.

End

TIP

Warp Speed

If you change a font size by dragging the bottom or corner selection points, keep in mind that you run a chance of distorting the type along with changing the type size. For greatest accuracy and no warping, enter the type size directly into the **Type Size** field.

CREATING A DROP SHADOW

You can add a drop shadow to text or a graphic element, and control exactly how that shadow looks and the way it falls.

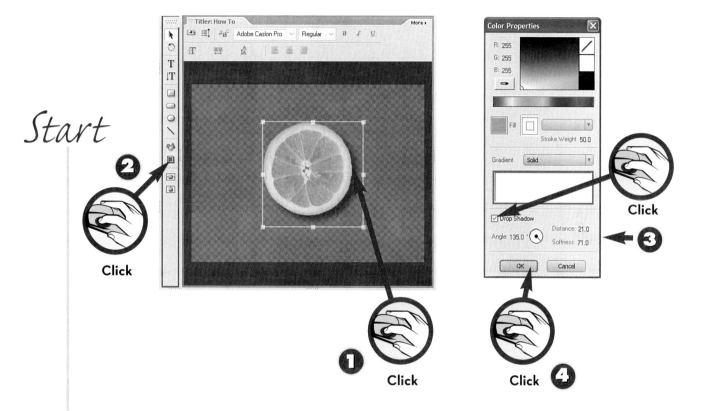

Start

Click

Click

Click

Click

End

1 In the Titler, select the text or object to which you want to apply a drop shadow (or for which you want to adjust the drop shadow).

2 Select the **Color Properties** button.

3 Click the **Drop Shadow** check box and adjust the shadow's Angle, Distance, and Softness settings.

4 Click **OK**.

TIP

Shadow Sense

Premiere Elements's drop shadow settings enable you to control how soft the shadow appears, the angle that it falls, and how far it falls from the text (or the graphic). Experiment to give your text just the right look. For a cleaner look, lose the shadow altogether by unchecking the **Drop Shadow** box.

ADJUSTING CHARACTER SPACING (KERNING)

Most likely, the spacing between the words and letters in the titles you create in Premiere Elements will look right. But there will be cases where you will want to tighten or loosen the spacing a bit for design reasons, to make the text fit in a certain space, or for other reasons.

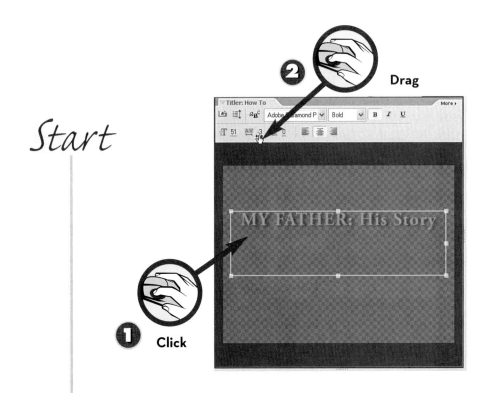

Start

2 Drag

1 Click

1 Select the text for which you want to adjust the word and character spacing (called *kerning*).

2 Drag your cursor in the **Kerning** field (labeled with AV and a left/right arrow) to adjust the kerning as needed (or type a value directly in the field).

End

> **NOTE**
>
> **Directional Signal**
>
> Drag your cursor to the left to tighten the kerning and to the right to loosen the kerning. *Tighten* means to bring the letters closer together; *loosen* means to add more space between them.

ADJUSTING PARAGRAPH SPACING (LEADING)

Depending on how much text is on the screen, you might need to decrease the *leading* (the space between paragraphs) a bit to make it fit. Conversely, you might find you want to increase the leading a bit for aesthetic reasons to make the text look better.

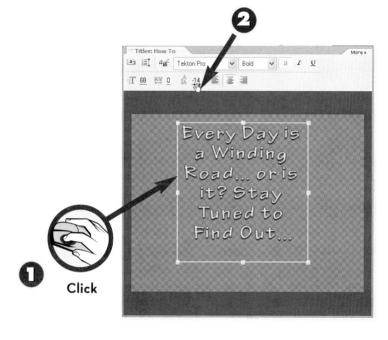

Click

1 Select the text for which you want to adjust the paragraph spacing.

2 Drag your cursor in the **Leading** field (labeled with *AA* and an up/down arrow) to adjust the leading as needed.

CREATING SCROLLING OR CRAWLING TEXT

At the end of most movies, you see the credits scroll across the screen, from the bottom of the screen to the top or vice versa. If you've seen Star Wars, you've seen one of the most famous scrolling credits. Crawling text, on the other hand, moves from left to right, or vice versa, across the screen. Premiere Elements provides you with the tools to create your own scrolling and crawling text.

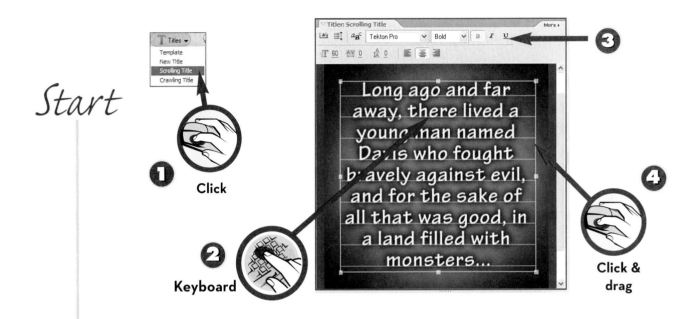

Start

Click

Keyboard

Click & drag

Long ago and far away, there lived a young man named Davis who fought bravely against evil, and for the sake of all that was good, in a land filled with monsters...

1 Click and hold the **Titles** button and select **Scrolling Title** or **Crawling Title**.

2 Type the text for your title on the screen.

3 Optionally, modify the font, font color, alignment, and other attributes for the text (refer to the tasks earlier in this chapter that show you how to make these changes).

4 Click and drag the text box to move the text into position on the screen, if necessary.

Continued

NOTE

The Longest Word

Because scrolling and crawling titles typically use lots of text, cut and paste text into a text box in the Titler in Premiere Elements by first creating your text in Microsoft Word or other word processor. Run a spell-check on the text before you bring it over to Premiere Elements. By the way, since Premiere Elements does not have a spell checker with the Titler, a great way to check your text is to copy and paste it into Word, run a spell check, and then copy and paste it back into Premiere Elements.

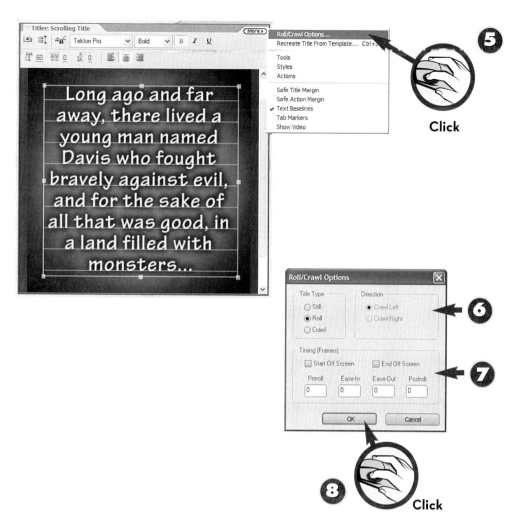

Click

Click

5 Click the **More** button, and choose **Roll/Crawl Options**.

6 You can modify the **Title Type** (Still, Roll, or Crawl) or the **Direction** for crawling titles.

7 You can also modify the **Timing** (in number of frames) for how the title appears on the screen and how it exits off screen.

8 When you're done, click **OK**.

End

ADDING A PICTURE TO THE TITLE

You can add a still picture to your title, in addition to any text. A clip art picture of a palm tree, for example, could add visual interest to a vacation title, as might a clip art teddy bear to a baby video title.

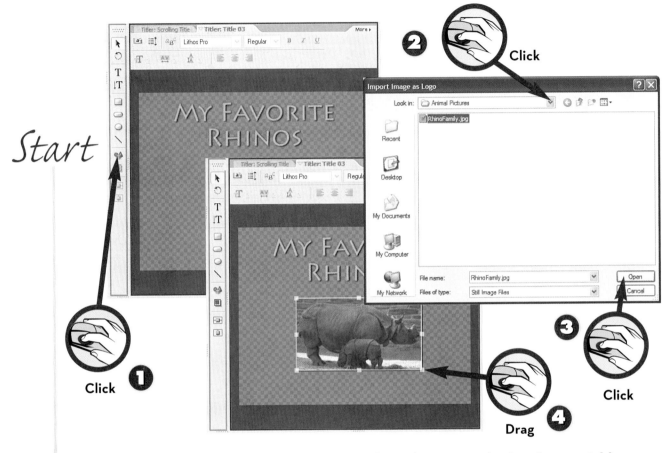

Start

Click

Click

Click

Drag

End

1 Click the **Add Image** button (or right-click on the Titles area and select **Image**, **Add Image**).

2 Click the **Look In** drop-down list to browse to locate and select the image you want to add.

3 Click **Open**.

4 After the image is placed in the window, you can drag a corner handle (small white square) to make the image larger or smaller (or right-click on the image and select **Transform**, **Scale** and enter a Scale [resize] amount and click OK).

ADDING SHAPES AS GRAPHIC ELEMENTS

Adding lines, boxes, and other graphic elements can add a professional touch to your graphics. A line between a title and a subtitle, for example, is a subtle but effective design technique. You could also add a semi-transparent box behind text to help make it more legible when it appears over a background that would otherwise make the text hard to read.

Start

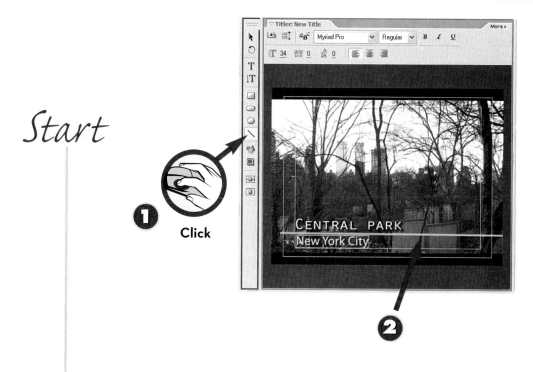

Click

1 Click on a graphic element: the square, the circle, or the line.

2 Draw the graphic at the location you want, and to the size and shape you want.

End

TIP
Change the Shape's Style
The styles in the Style palette work on shapes exactly like they do on text. Click on any style to apply the new style to the shape. To change a shape's color, click the **Color Properties** button.

TIP
Shape Rotation
You can rotate shapes just like text. Use the **Rotation tool** or right-click and select **Transform**, **Rotation** to use the Rotation dialog box.

ARRANGING TEXT AND GRAPHICS

Premiere Elements provides a number of handy tools for lining up text and graphics and moving them around so they line up in front and in back of each other as well.

Start

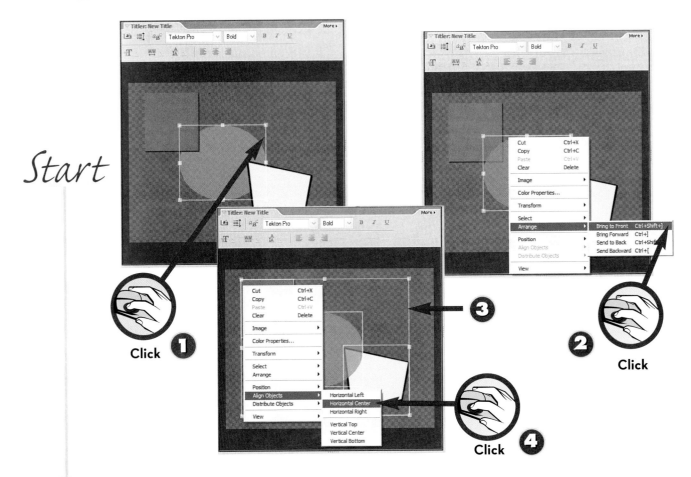

Click **1**

Click **2**

3

Click **4**

1 Select the text and graphic object(s) you want to relocate.

2 Right-click and select from the options available under **Arrange** in the contextual menu to move objects back and forth; for example, to bring an object to the front.

3 Select multiple objects by shift-clicking on them or by dragging the mouse across a group of objects to select the objects using a marquee box.

4 Then right-click and from the contextual menu, select to **Position**, **Transform**, **Align Objects**, or **Distribute Objects** to move and align objects horizontally and vertically.

End

TIP

Can't Click It?

If you can't click on an object that is sitting behind another object, right-click on the object that's in the way and choose **Select**, **Next Object Below** from the contextual menu. Other Select submenu choices might help you out in similar situations as well.

ADDING A TITLE TO THE TIMELINE

After you have a title all set to go, you just need to drag-and-drop it onto the Timeline to include it in your movie.

Start

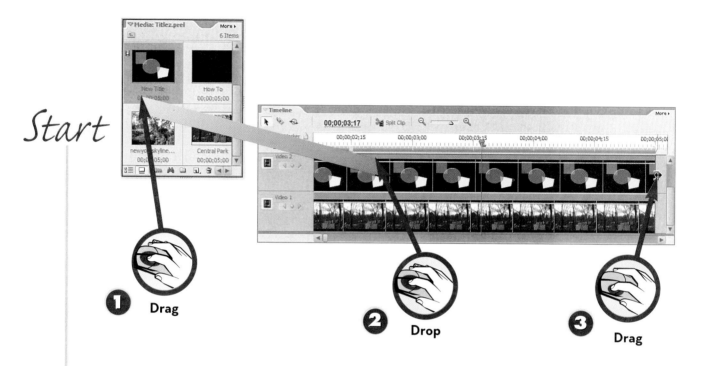

1 Drag

2 Drop

3 Drag

1 Drag a title that you want to use from the **Media** panel.

2 Drop it on to the position on the track where you want it to be, above the video track where you want it to appear.

3 Optionally, stretch the title as needed so it displays as needed.

End

THE BASICS OF SPECIAL EFFECTS

By having an understanding of how to use effects and by learning how to use the more essential effects in Adobe Premiere Elements, you will be able to make changes to your clips as needed to achieve some amazing cinematic effects.

Basic effects include changing a color clip to black and white or to a single color tone (such as sepia, to give the clip an old film look); giving a clip a 1960s look by solarizing it; blurring a clip; or distorting a clip in other ways. You can transform the shape of a clip by making it look like a trapezoid or parallelogram. You can apply any effect to a clip and undo it, as you need. You can also copy the effects on one clip and apply them to another clip, which is very handy if you've created a great effect on a clip and want to use it elsewhere. (Better still is saving your effects as your own Presets.)

All in all, with the basic set of effects available to you with Premiere Elements 2.0, you can go all Hollywood on your video clips and have almost too much fun while you're doing it.

BASIC EFFECTS ARE HANDY EFFECTS

Change the look and shape of any video clip for dramatic effect.

From this...

...to this (mirrored, transformed, and beveled)!

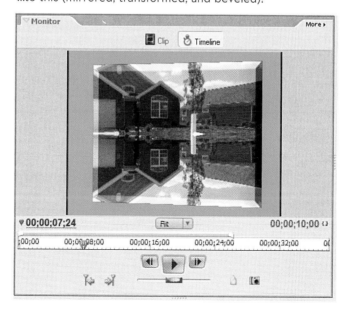

APPLYING A PRESET EFFECT

Premiere Elements includes a number of preset effects you apply by dragging and dropping them onto any video or still image clip on the Timeline. Adobe has determined that these Presets are some of the most common and most useful effects anyone would want to apply and has made them very easy to use.

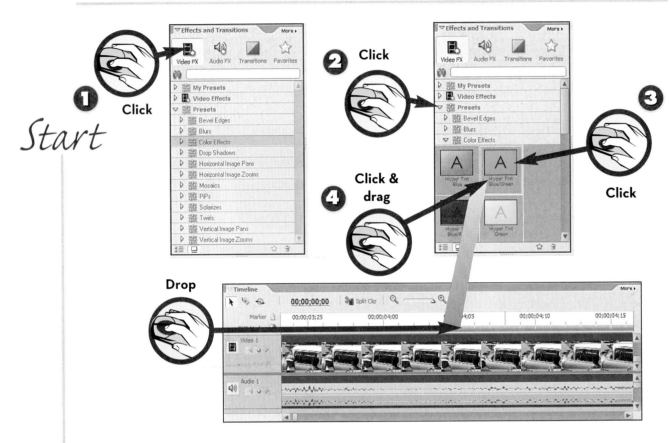

1. Click the **Video FX** button on the Effects and Transitions panel.

2. Click the arrow next to any of the 12 effect categories under the **Presets** area to see the available effects.

3. Select the Video FX preset you want to use.

4. Drag and drop the effect onto a clip on the **Timeline**.

End

TIP

Monitoring the Monitor

You can see the results of an effect in the Monitor panel as you apply the effect to a clip. In most cases, effects appear in the Monitor panel instantly. In other cases, the effect won't be obvious in the Monitor panel until after you've made adjustments in the Properties panel. In still other cases, the effect won't be visible until you click the **Play** button on the Monitor panel.

SAVING YOUR SETTINGS AS A PRESET

When you drag and drop any effect onto a clip on the Timeline, the settings for that effect instantly appear in the Properties panel so you can make adjustments. Your adjustments aren't automatically saved, however. But if you tweak a particular effect to your liking and want to save it for use again, save it as a Preset in the My Presets folder on the Effects and Transitions panel.

Start

Right-click

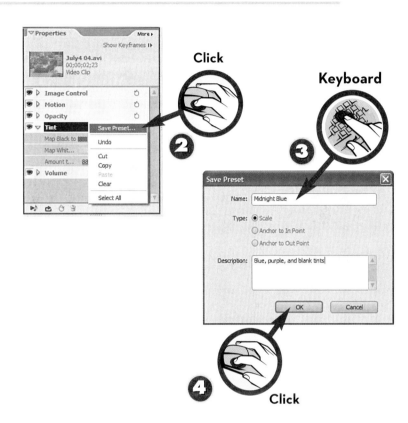

Click

Keyboard

Click

1. Right-click on the name of the effect you want to save in the Properties panel.

2. From the contextual menu, select **Save Preset**.

3. In the Save Preset dialog, modify the default name with a more descriptive name you'll remember and give the preset an optional description.

4. Click **OK** to save your new preset.

End

NOTE

My Presets

Your saved preset appears in the My Presets area of the Effects and Transitions panel, at the top of the list of effects and transitions.

NOTE

Saving a Preset's Settings

You can save a saved preset as a new preset. If you apply one of your saved presets, make some changes to its settings, and like these new settings, too, save these settings as a new preset.

RENDERING AN EFFECT

An effect is only simulated until you render the effect. To render an effect after you have applied it to a clip, click on the Timeline and press the **Enter** key.

Start

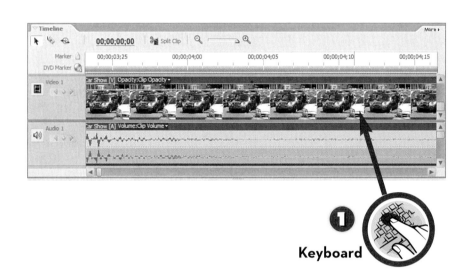

Keyboard

1 Apply an effect to a clip in the Timeline as described in "Applying a Preset Effect," and then press the **Enter** key on your keyboard.

Continued

-CAUTION

An Enter Key Caveat

The Enter key in Premiere Elements almost exclusively has the job of rendering effects and transitions on the Timeline. However, if there is nothing to render or your cursor is in a window that also uses the Enter key, such as the Monitor panel, a different action might occur instead, such as the video being played.

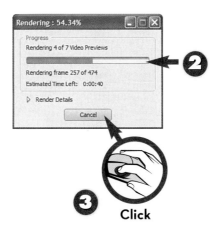

2

3 Click

2 The Rendering dialog alerts you of progress and other bits of information.

3 Click **Cancel** if you want to stop the render early. Any clip rendered up to that point on the Timeline is finished; the other clips not yet rendered have to wait until next time. (Premiere Elements will automatically pick up where it left off.)

End

NOTE

Look for the Red

If any clip on the Timeline has a red line running above it for the full length of the clip, this is Premiere Elements's indicator that the clip has not yet been rendered. So until the effects have been applied (rendered), what you are seeing as you work on your movie is Premiere Elements's pretty good approximation of what that effect will ultimately look like.

COPYING THE EFFECTS FROM ONE CLIP TO ANOTHER

After you have applied an effect or set of effects to a clip, you might find that those same settings would work well on another clip. With Premiere Elements, you don't need to redo all the tweaking you did for the original clip—just copy those settings over to the next clip!

Click

1 Right-click on the clip whose effects you want to copy and select **Copy** from the contextual menu.

Continued

Continued

TIP

Less Is More, and More Is Less

To delete an effect from a clip, highlight the effect's name in the Properties panel and press the Backspace key on your keyboard, or right-click on the effect and select **Cut** or **Clear** from the contextual menu. You can also use the **More** button on the Properties panel and select **Delete Selected Effect**. To remove all of the effects applied to a given clip, select **Delete All Effects from Clip** instead.

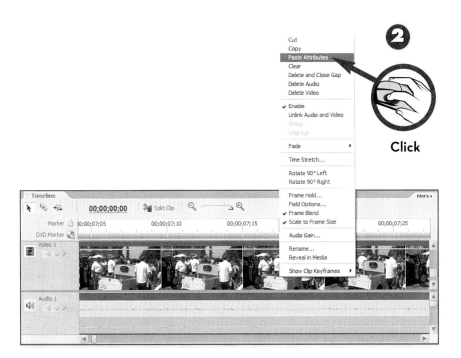

Cut
Copy
Paste Attributes
Clear
Delete and Close Gap
Delete Audio
Delete Video

✓ Enable
Unlink Audio and Video
Group
Ungroup

Fade ▸

Time Stretch...

Rotate 90° Left
Rotate 90° Right

Frame Hold...
Field Options...
✓ Frame Blend
✓ Scale to Frame Size

Audio Gain...

Rename...
Reveal in Media

Show Clip Keyframes ▸

Click

2 Right-click on the clip to which you want to copy the effects and select **Paste Attributes** from the contextual menu.

End

SEARCHING FOR AN EFFECT

Premiere Elements provides you with an effective tool for finding the effect you're looking for without clicking your way through all of the various categories and subcategories on the Effects and Transitions panel.

Start

Keyboard

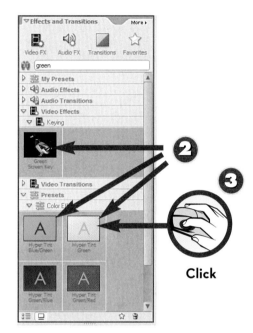

Click

① To find a particular effect, click in the **Find** box (next to the binoculars) and start typing the name of the effect.

② As you type, Premiere Elements presents any and all effects that contain that letter or group of letters as part of their name.

③ Select the effect you want from those displayed.

End

NOTE

Everything Is Everything

When you use Premiere Elements's search function, Premiere Elements finds not just video effects, but everything in the Effects and Transitions panel with the letters or name you type, including presets (including any that you've created), audio effects, and audio and video transitions.

USING TRANSPARENCY WITH CLIPS

You can use transparency (or lack of opacity, to use Premiere Elements terms) to reveal underlying clips on the Timeline and add an interesting effect.

Start

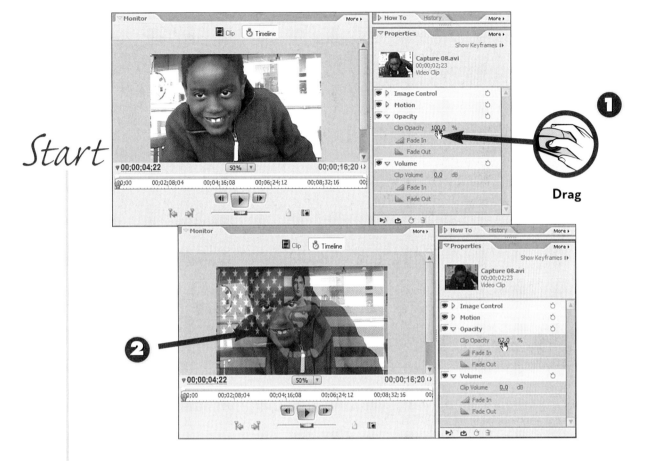

Drag

1 Open the Properties panel of a selected clip and adjust the **Clip Opacity** number.

2 As you adjust the opacity by using the slider or typing in a new amount, more or less of the underlying clip shows through.

End

TIP
We All Live with a Yellow Rubberband...
You can adjust the transparency of a clip by moving the yellow rubberband on the Timeline. Be sure that Opacity is selected first. The problem with this method is that you can't view your changes in the Monitor panel as you make them.

TIP
Time to Be Transparent
Fade a clip using the options on the Properties panel. To have the visible clip fade and reveal the clip beneath it, select **Fade In**. To have the visible clip fade out at the end and have the clip below fade in, click **Fade Out**.

CHANGING A CLIP'S SIZE

If you want to create a smaller or larger size for a given clip for effect, it's easy to do in Premiere Elements.

Start

① Double-click

② Click & drag

① Double-click on the selected clip from the Timeline in the **Monitor panel**. (A circle with a cross appears at the center of the image.)

② Click any one of the four corners of the image and drag to resize the clip.

End

TIP

Changing a Clip's Size Numerically

You can more accurately change the size of a clip using the Scale control on the Properties panel. In the Properties panel for the clip, double-click **Motion** and adjust the **Scale** up or down.

TIP

Changing a Clip's Size Rubberband-ly

You can also change the size of a clip using the yellow rubberband version of the Scale control on the Timeline. Select the clip. Select **Motion**, **Scale** from the clip's Timeline menu. Then drag the rubberband slowly up or down to change the clip's size.

TRANSFORMING A CLIP'S SHAPE

You can transform a clip so it is more of a trapezoid than a rectangle if that suits your project's needs. You can also clip or crop the clip, flip it horizontally or vertically, or create an effect where it looks as if the television you're viewing has reception problems.

Start

Drag & drop ❶

❷

❶ Select a **Transform** effect from and the Effects and Transitions panel and drag and drop it onto a clip on the Timeline.

❷ At this point you can adjust the effect's settings in the Properties panel or the effect's Settings dialog, if one is available for your chosen effect. (If you use a Settings dialog, click **OK** when you're done to accept the new settings.)

End

NOTE

Spy Versus Spy
If you are creating an action movie, or a parody of one, you can create a clip to represent a badly received video transmission using the Vertical Hold effect or the Roll effect, or a combination of the two.

SHARPENING OR BLURRING A CLIP

With Premiere Elements, you can make clips a bit blurry or a bit crisper (sharper), according to your needs. You can also make a clip extremely blurry or sharp and even add an eerie ghost effect, perfect for Halloween party videos.

Start

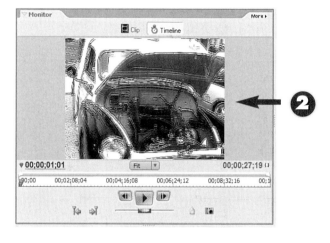

Drag & drop

1. Select a **Blur and Sharpen** effect from the Effects and Transitions panel and drag and drop the effect onto a clip in the Timeline.
2. At this point you can also adjust the clip's parameters in the Properties panel to further refine the effect, if available.

End

TIP

A Ghost of Your Former Clip

Ghosting is an extreme form of blurriness, but it's also extremely cool and fun to use. You use it to simulate sickness, dizziness, or mystery. Just apply the Ghost effect to a clip and Premiere Elements makes multiple transparent copies of the images in the clip, giving an almost hallucinogenic effect of spirits in the night (all night). Echo creates a similar effect; give that a try, too (select **Time**, **Echo**).

CREATING A WATERCOLOR LOOK

You can give your video the look of a watercolor painting using Premiere Elements's Facet effect, which is located under the Pixelate section of Video Effects.

Start

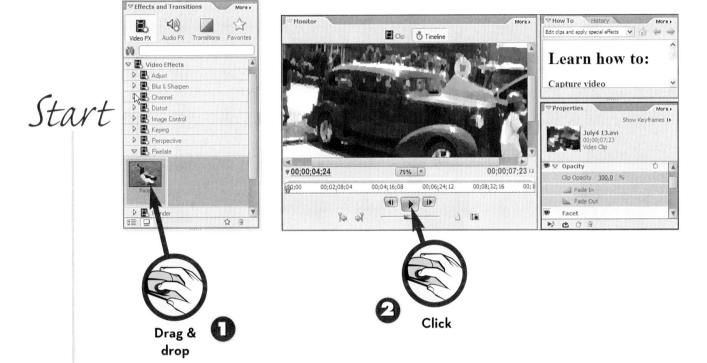

Drag & drop ❶

❷ **Click**

❶ From the **Pixelate** category in the Video Effects category of the Effects and Transitions panel, select the **Facet** effect and drag and drop it onto a clip on the Timeline.

❷ Click the **Play** button in the Monitor panel to see the Facet (watercolor) effect. (Or better yet, press the **Enter** key on your keyboard to render the effect.)

End

TIP

Different Facets for Different Folks

The Facet effect is subtle and has no controls in the Properties panel. You may find that some clips, due to the colors and level of detail, work better with this effect than others. For example, this effect works especially well with garden scenes. You can increase the watercolor effect by dragging and dropping the Facet effect multiple times onto the same clip.

STYLIZING YOUR CLIPS

Premiere Elements provides you with 10 effects that each change a clip in a different stylistic way. Each of these effects can add something unique to your video project.

Start

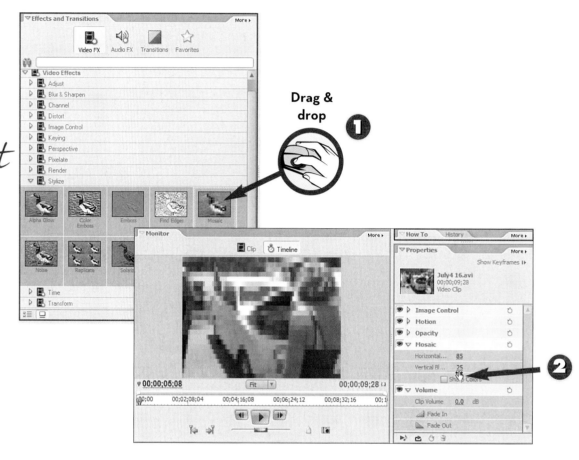

Drag & drop **1**

2

1 Select a **Stylize** effect in the Video Effects category of the Effects and Transitions panel and drag and drop it onto a clip on the Timeline.

2 At this point, you can also adjust the settings for the effect in the Properties panel, if desired.

End

NOTE

Style Council

Under the Stylize heading for Video Effects panel you'll find 10 effects including Alpha Glow, Color Emboss, Emboss, Find Edges, Mosaic, Noise, Replicate, Solarize, Strobe Light, and Texturize.

TIP

Create a 1960s Effect

Apply the **Solarize** effect to a clip and set the Threshold on the Properties panel into the 90s for a flashback to the '60s. Add some Hendrix, Stones, or the Who to your soundtrack and your backyard barbeque video just became Woodstock! Don't bogart that bratwurst!

CREATING PERSPECTIVE EFFECTS

You can twist and turn your clips every which way but loose with Premiere Elements. You can also add a drop shadow and a bevel edge, should you so desire. All these effects are available in the Perspective category of the Premiere Elements's video effects.

Start

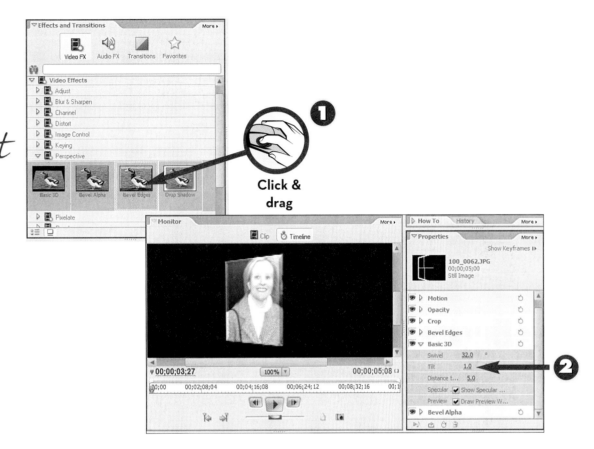

Click & drag

① Select one of the **Perspective** effects in the Video Effects category of the Effects and Transitions panel and drag and drop it onto a clip on the Timeline.

② At this point you can also adjust the settings for the effect in the Properties panel, if you want to change the look of the effect.

End

NOTE

A New Perspective

The Perspective category is a bit of a misnomer for the effects you'll find here. If you want to give a clip a beveled or framed effect, here's where you'll find it. Here, too, is where you'll find Premiere Elements's drop shadow effect.

USING THE DISTORT EFFECTS

The Distort effects are similar to other Premiere Elements effects that allow you to transform your clips geometrically. However, the Distort effects also give you the ability to ripple, bend, mirror, and distort. Think of these as the fun house mirror effects of Adobe Premiere Elements.

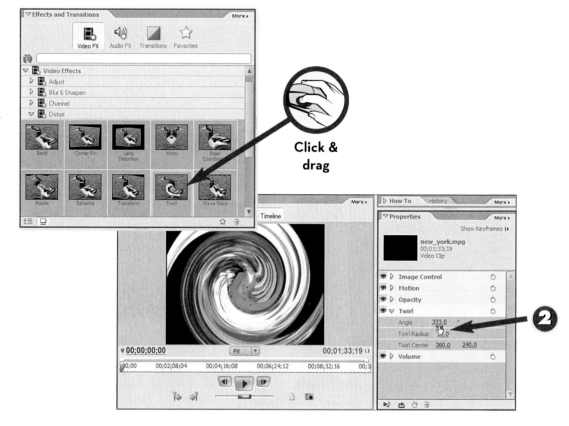

Click & drag

Select one of the Distort effects in the Video Effects category of the Effects and Transitions panel and drag and drop it onto a clip on the Timeline.

**At this point you can adjust the settings for the effect in the Properties panel, if you want to change the look of the effect.

End

MAKING A CLIP LOOK LIKE A BLACK-AND-WHITE MOVIE

Black-and-white movies are a classic form of the art, a cinemagraphic style used by some of our most respected directors. You can use it, too, if your story requires it. It's especially effective if you are telling a story that takes place in the past.

Start

Click & drag **①**

Before

After

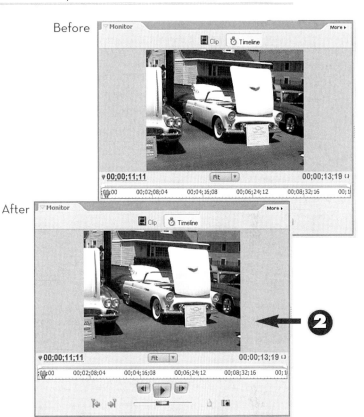

②

① Drag the **Black & White** effect from the Image Control category in the Video Effects category of the Effects and Transitions panel and drop it onto a clip on the Timeline.

② View the results in the Monitor window.

End

NOTE

Creating a Single-Color Effect (Tinting)
After you've converted a clip to black and white, you can easily tint it by dropping the Tint effect on the clip and selecting the colors to substitute for either black or white or both.

TIP

A World Without Color
For another cool effect (which can be used when you want to create a horror or shocking scene in your movie), try applying the Extract effect in the Adjust section of the Video Effects. It completely removes all of the color from a clip.

ADVANCED EFFECTS TECHNIQUES

Premiere Elements's advanced special effects enable you to create green screen (chroma key) effects where you can remove the background from a clip and replace it with stock footage of Mt. Everest, for example. Look, Ma, I've summited! You can also pan across a picture, Ken Burns style, or zoom in or out on a video clip as it plays. You can create picture-in-picture effects, just like you've seen in the movies, where multiple video clips are tiled across the screen (this might soon become known as the 24 effect, as that popular television show is perhaps the one best known for using this technique). You can add an artificial lens flare to a clip to make it look as if the sun shone too brightly onto a reflective object in the scene. Or, you can even apply fake lightning to create your own Frankenstein movie. Premiere Elements includes effects that are both serious and fun to help you make the movie you have envisioned.

If you like to tweak, you're in luck. Some advanced special effects such as PiP, Image Pan, and the lightening effect have almost endless settings and adjustments for you to modify. But if you prefer your effects "as is," Premiere Elements's effects work fine right off the shelf. You can use the effects just as they are to begin. Then, as you become more proficient with the software, you can explore the customization possibilities for the effects and gain even more control over keyframes, motion settings, and things such as interpolation and Bézier curves. For now, just enjoy the professional look that Premiere Elements's advanced effects can give your video projects and have fun.

HOLLYWOOD AT THE CLICK OF A BUTTON

Add brilliant effects to your movies as easy as you can say, "Action!"

STACKING MULTIPLE EFFECTS

Effects in Premiere Elements can (and should) be used by themselves. However, effects, when used together, can create interesting and useful effects not achievable by any one single effect alone.

Start

Drag & drop

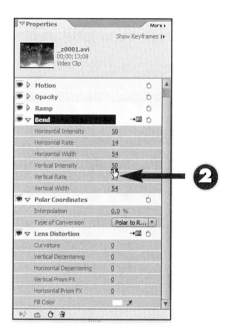

① Apply effects from the **Video Effects** category of the Effects and Transitions panel by dragging and dropping them one at a time onto the same clip in the Timeline.

② Optionally adjust each effect's settings on the **Properties panel**.

End

NOTE

More of the Same

Apply the same effect to a clip multiple times to achieve interesting effects. For each instance of the effect, change the settings. Each instance is rendered, but the result is an overall effect not achievable by using the effect just once.

TIP

Render When Ready

When you apply an effect, Premiere Elements approximates how it will look. A red bar appears at the top of the clip. After you render an effect (by pressing the **Enter** key), the effect looks better and the red bar turns to green.

REORDERING EFFECTS

Effects work differently when stacked (combined) depending upon the order that they're stacked. In other words, an effect has a different effect on a clip depending on whether it's first in the stack or last.

Start

Drag

Here, the Mirror effect is applied first, and then the Horizontal Flip effect.

Here, the Horizontal Flip effect is applied first, and then the Mirror effect.

1 Stack effects as described previously in the "Stacking Multiple Effects" task.

2 Then, reposition each effect in the **Properties panel** by dragging effects up or down in the list.

End

NOTE

Strange Effects

Changing the order of effects doesn't always have a dramatic, or even any, effect on the clip. But sometimes the result can be very different. When you are using more than one effect on a clip, experiment with the order of the effects to get the results you want.

CREATING A PICTURE-IN-PICTURE (PIP) EFFECT

Creating a PiP (Picture-in-Picture) effect—where an additional video (or videos) appears in a small window overlaid on the main video—is remarkably easy to do in Premiere Elements.

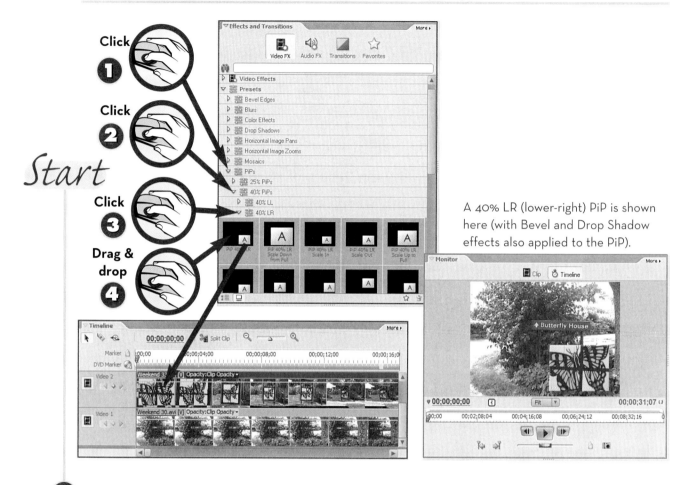

A 40% LR (lower-right) PiP is shown here (with Bevel and Drop Shadow effects also applied to the PiP).

① On the Effects and Transitions panel, under Presets, click the triangle next to **PiPs**.

② Click the triangle next to one of the PiP size groups (such as **40% PiPs**).

③ Click the triangle next to one of the PiP directional groups (such as **40% LR**).

④ With at least two tracks of video on the Timeline, drag and drop a PiP effect onto a video clip on a higher track.

End

NOTE

The Dozens

Dozens of PiP effects are available to you with Premiere Elements—there are 23 PiPs in the 40% LR section alone. These include static as well as motion effects, where the PiP window spins or slides across the screen.

TIP

Easy Customization

If the default location for a PiP isn't exactly where you want it, double-click the **PiP window** in the Monitor panel and drag the PiP window to another position. You can also add additional effects to the PiP window.

PANNING ACROSS A CLIP

You can create the effect of the camera slowly panning across a picture or a video clip in Premiere Elements (what's become known as the Ken Burns effect). You can set whether the pan moves horizontally or vertically, as well as its speed and other options.

Start

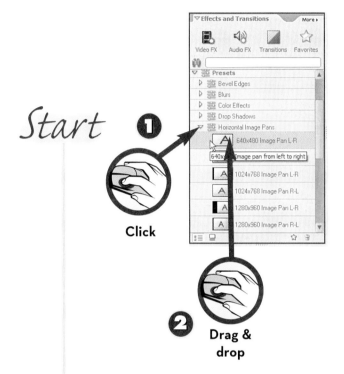

Click

2 Drag & drop

3 Click

1 On the Effects and Transitions panel, click the triangle next to **Presets** and then select either **Horizontal Image Pans** or **Vertical Image Pans**.

2 Drag and drop a pan effect to a video clip on the Timeline.

3 On the **Monitor** panel, optionally click on the clip and drag the points to adjust the path of the pan, as needed.

End

TIP

There Will Be a Test

Test the pan effect you selected by playing the clip in the Monitor panel. If it's not quite what you wanted, click the **Undo** button and try another one. Premiere Elements ships with so many pan effects that you're sure to find one that suits your needs.

ZOOMING IN AND OUT ON A CLIP

An effective camera technique while shooting is the zoom, when used appropriately. With Premiere Elements, you can re-create the effect of the camera zooming in on a scene or zooming back out.

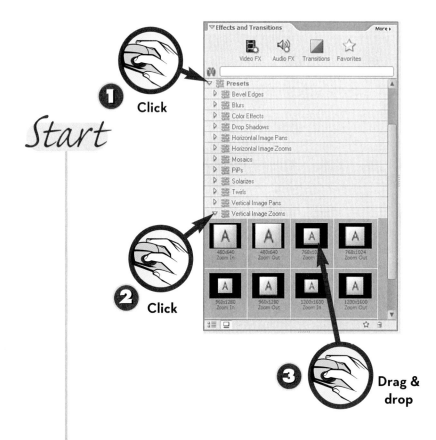

Start

Drag & drop

A clip at the start of a 768 x 1024 Zoom In.

1 On the Effects and Transitions panel, click the triangle next to **Presets**.

2 Click the triangle next to either **Horizontal Image Zooms** or **Vertical Image Zooms**.

3 Drag and drop a zoom effect to a video clip on the Timeline.

End

ADDING A LENS FLARE TO A CLIP

A *lens flare* is the effect of a bright light, almost always the sun, causing a bright reflection on the camera lens. Lens flares can add a bit of realism to a clip, especially if you have a still image of a car in the desert, for example. Adding a lens flare and panning across the image gives the illusion that it isn't a photograph but a video clip.

Start

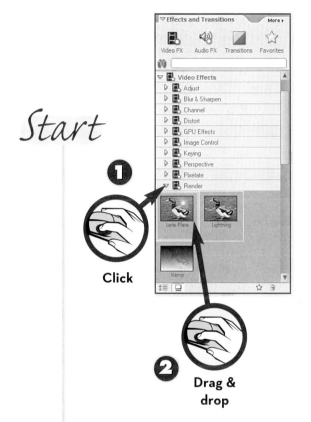

Click

Drag & drop

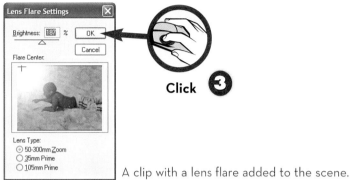

Click **3**

A clip with a lens flare added to the scene.

1 On the Effects and Transitions panel, click the triangle next to **Render**.

2 Drag and drop the **Lens Flare** effect to a video clip on the Timeline.

3 On the Lens Flare Settings window, make adjustments as needed such as moving the lens flare's location or selecting a lens flare type, and click **OK**.

End

NOTE

Plenty of Flare

Each of the lens flare types available at the bottom of the Lens Flare Settings window gives you a slightly different type of lens flare. For example, the 105mm Prime lens flare is intensely white and large. The 35mm Prime has a more bluish tint. And the 50-300mm Zoom lens flare gives you the added effect of additional halos on the screen. Note that you can make additional adjustments to the lens flare using the settings on the Properties panel.

ADDING LIGHTNING TO A CLIP

You can add lightning to a clip of a night scene or a stormy scene using Premiere Elements's Lightning effect.

Start

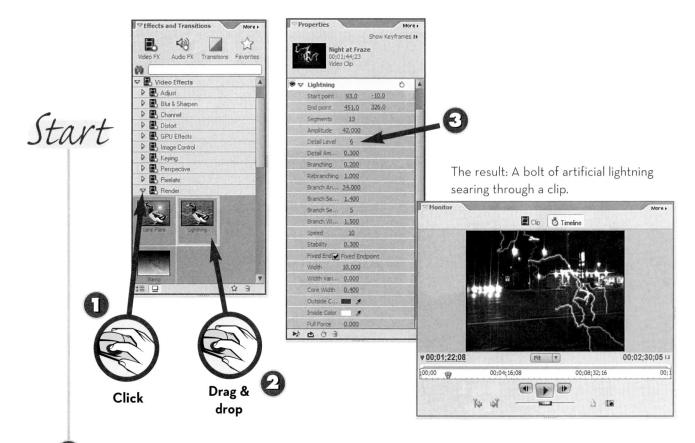

The result: A bolt of artificial lightning searing through a clip.

1 On the Effects and Transitions panel, click the triangle next to **Render**.

2 Drag and drop the **Lightning** effect to a video clip on the Timeline.

3 Optionally, you can adjust the effect's settings on the **Properties panel**.

End

NOTE

That's a Lot of Settings!

The Lightning effect has perhaps more settings than any other effect in Premiere Elements. However, they are all easy to understand if you think of a bolt of lightning like a tree with branches. Experiment with these different settings to achieve different effects, such as the Frankenstein's laboratory effect of lightning in the lab.

ADVANCED VIDEO TRICKS USING THE GPU EFFECTS

Premiere Elements's GPU effects are very computer-graphics intensive and as such they require a graphics display board in your computer with a graphics processing unit (GPU). How do you know if you have this capability? Simple: If the GPU effects don't show up in your list of Video Effects, you don't have it!

Start

Click

Drag & drop

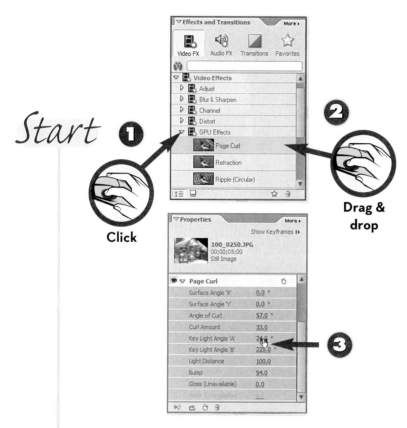

A clip with the Page Curl effect applied.

① On the Effects and Transitions panel, click the triangle next to **GPU Effects** and then select a GPU effect such as Page Curl.

② Drag and drop the GPU effect to a video clip on the **Timeline**.

③ Optionally, you can adjust the effect's settings on the **Properties panel**.

End

TIP

A Different Way of Seeing

You can view effects in a list to see more effects at one time. To switch to list view, click the **List View** button at the bottom-left corner of the Effects and Transitions panel. To switch back, click the **Thumbnail View** button.

TIP

Hardware Acceleration

If your graphics card settings for hardware acceleration are off or set low, this disables the GPU. Check your settings by selecting **Start**, **Control Panel**, **Display**. Select the **Settings** tab and then click on the **Advanced** button.

CHROMA KEYS AND GREEN SCREENS

Chroma keys and screens refer to the process of filming someone against a solid color background and then keying out that background, which is typically green or blue, and substituting a video clip or image for that background. This gives the effect of the person standing in front of the Taj Mahal, a busy city intersection, or in the middle of the woods, when in fact they were simply standing in a room in your house in front of a green sheet.

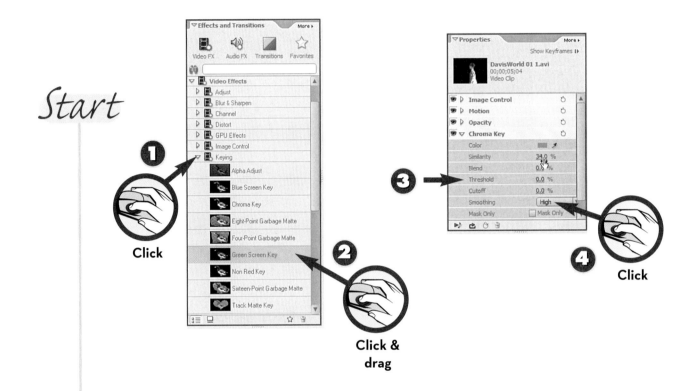

Start

Click

Click & drag

Click

1. On the Effects and Transitions panel, select **Keying** from the Video Effects category.

2. Depending on the background your clip has (blue, green, or other color), select a key type and drag it to the Timeline onto a green screen clip.

3. Optionally, you can modify the settings in the **Properties panel** for the effect.

4. If the foreground image looks a little rough, select a **Smoothing** setting of Low or High.

Continued

TIP

Chroma Chameleon

The Blue Screen Key and the Green Screen Key are used for very specific values of blue and green. If you used a blue or green background that doesn't seem to be working with these keys, select **Chroma Key** instead and then use the Eye Dropper tool to select the background color from the clip in the Monitor panel. This way, virtually any solid color background will work!

The green screen video clip.

The world traveler in England.

The world traveler again, at Yosemite National Park.

5 There are a variety of results you can achieve using this effect.

End

MOTION EFFECTS AND KEYFRAMES

Premiere Elements includes sophisticated motion effects with keyframes that are easy to use once you get the hang of it. Motion effects enable you to spin or toss video clips or images, such as a logo, across the screen.

Start

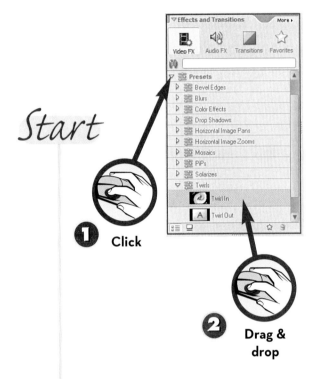

① Click

② Drag & drop

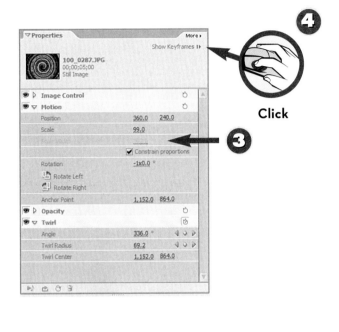

③

④ Click

① On the Effects and Transitions panel, click the triangle next to **Presets** and select a motion effect such as Twirl or one of the Pan or Zoom effects.

② Drag and drop the effect onto a clip on the Timeline.

③ Optionally, you can adjust the Motion settings on the **Properties panel**.

④ You can also add keyframes by clicking **Show Keyframes** to open the keyframe panel of the Properties panel.

Continued

NOTE

The Key to It All

Keyframes allow you to control when the action stops, starts, or changes. You pick the exact frame where the effect starts, for example. This is called a *keyframe*. All of the zoom and pan effects can use keyframes that you can set using the Motion settings on the Properties panel.

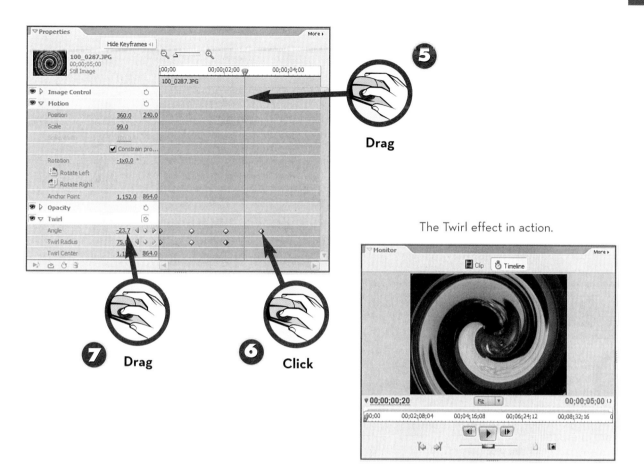

The Twirl effect in action.

Drag

Drag

Click

5 Drag the CTI to the point in the clip where you want to add a keyframe to the clip.

6 Click the **diamond-shaped icon** next to Angle or Twirl Radius to add a new keyframe at the location of the CTI.

7 Adjust the **Angle** or **Twirl Radius** setting for that keyframe by dragging in the number field or typing a new setting.

End

TIP

Kind of a Drag

You can adjust the timing between key events by dragging the keyframe icons on the Timeline to lengthen or shorten the distance between keyframes. You can also delete any unnecessary keyframes using the same button you use to add a new keyframe.

PREMIERE ELEMENTS'S BUILT-IN VIDEO REPAIR TOOLS

Unless you happen to own the very best camcorder, shoot under optimal lighting conditions, and have your camcorder options set perfectly, chances are that the video you shoot will, at least occasionally, need a little help. Fear not. After you get back to your studio, Premiere Elements has a number of very effective and (for the most part) easy-to-use effects that act like filters to improve the look of any video clip.

Premiere Elements filter effects have been specifically designed to correct color, brightness, and contrast problems with video clips. In fact, they are the same filters available in Adobe's professional video-editing software, Premiere Pro.

Have fun applying the filter effects—you can create some astonishing and weird effects with your clips. But be aware that tweaking the video clips you are trying to fix can sometimes cause worse problems than those you are trying to correct! Don't worry, though; everything you do in Premiere Elements can easily be undone.

FIX YOUR CLIPS!

Multiple filters effects, each with numerous settings that you can adjust, give you the tools you need to handle virtually any color, brightness, or contrast nightmare you encounter and calm any clip down to more soothing tones.

From this...

...to this!

APPLYING A VIDEO EFFECT TO A CLIP

You apply Premiere Elements' effects in one of two ways. You drag and drop the effect from the Effects and Transitions panel onto the clip in the Timeline. Or you can select the clip first, and drag and drop the effect directly into the Properties panel. Either way, you make adjustments to the effect using the Properties panel.

Start

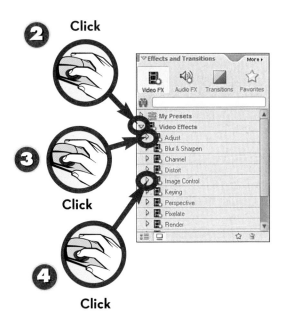

① On the Effects and Transitions panel, click the **Video FX** button. (*FX*, by the way, is industry shorthand for *effects*.)

② Click on the arrow next to the **Video Effects** heading to view the list of effects.

③ To select the effect you need, click on the arrow next to the **Adjust** subfolder, or...

④ Click on the arrow next to the **Image Control** subfolder.

Continued

TIP

We All Need Some Effection

The Adjust subfolder contains the following image correction effects: Auto Color, Auto Contrast, Auto Levels, Brightness and Contrast, the Channel Mixer, the Image Mixer, and the Shadows Highlight effect (along with two special effects filters discussed elsewhere in this book). The Image Control subfolder contains the Color Balance (HLS), the Color Balance (RGB), and the Gamma Correction effects. This subfolder, too, has additional special effects that are discussed elsewhere in this book.

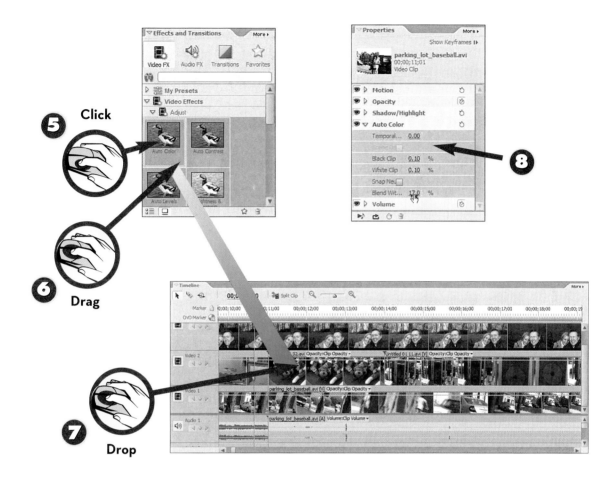

Click ⑤

⑥ **Drag**

⑦ **Drop**

⑧

⑤ Select the effect you want from those available in either the **Adjust** folder or the **Video Effects** folder.

⑥ Drag the effect to the **Timeline**.

⑦ Drop it on the clip you want to fix.

⑧ Fine-tune the effect using the controls on the Properties panel.

End

TIP

Make It Go Away!

Hide an effect by clicking the eye next the effect's name in the Properties panel for the clip. To see the effect, click the blank area where the eye *used* to be. *Delete* an effect by selecting it and clicking the garbage can icon.

TIP

Make It Stay!

You can save any changes you make in the Properties panel as brand new color effects. This is good because you can spend a lot of time getting effects just right. To do so, right-click on the effect name and select **Save Preset**.

CORRECTING VIDEO PROBLEMS USING THE AUTO COLOR, AUTO CONTRAST, AND AUTO LEVEL EFFECTS

Auto Color brings a clip into the middle range when it's too dark or bright. Auto Contrast adjusts the overall contrast between light and dark. Auto Levels adjusts a clip's highlights and can lighten areas of shadow.

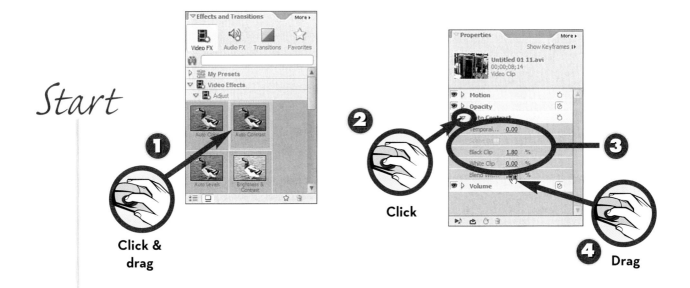

Start

Click & drag

Click

Drag

1. Drag and drop the **Auto Color**, **Auto Contrast**, or **Auto Levels** effect on to a clip in the Timeline.

2. On the **Properties panel**, click the arrow to the left of the effect name to see the controls.

Continued

TIP

Blending In
The more you blend the effect with the clip using the **Blend With Original** control, the less you'll see the effect. In other words, 0% will have the most noticeable impact on the clip, and 100% will have the least impact.

Before...

After...

Adjust the settings in the Properties panel as required for the best results with any given clip. The options vary with each effect, so you will want to experiment with each one to find just the right result.

Drag your mouse to the left or right on the **Blend With Original** control to increase or decrease how much of the effect is applied to the clip.

End

TIP

Scrub It

If the clip you want to work with is not currently displayed in the Monitor window, drag the **CTI** (Current Time Indicator) and scrub your way over to the clip on the Timeline until you see it in the Monitor window. Now you can make your color adjustments!

ADJUSTING A CLIP'S BRIGHTNESS AND CONTRAST LEVELS

One of the more common problems with a video clip is with its brightness and contrast. Often a clip is too bright or not bright enough, or there is too little or too much contrast. You make adjustments to a clip's brightness and contrast using the Brightness and Contrast effect.

Start

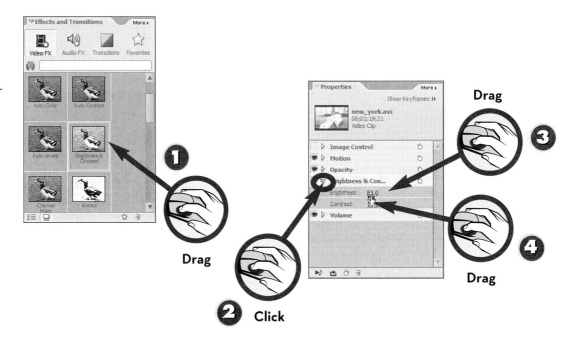

1 Drag and drop the **Brightness and Contrast** effect from the Adjust folder in the Effects and Transitions panel to a clip on the Timeline.

2 Click the arrow to the left of the **Brightness and Contrast** effect in the Properties panel to reveal its controls.

3 Drag your mouse to the left or right on the **Brightness** control to increase or decrease the clip's brightness.

4 Drag your mouse to the left or right on the **Contrast** control to increase or decrease the clip's contrast.

Continued

Before...

After...

5 The result is a much clearer shot with all the details standing out nicely.

End

TIP

Taking Control

The **Image Control** effect is another way you can adjust brightness and contrast. Even better, the **Image Control** effect enables you to adjust two additional color options at the same time: hue and saturation.

NOTE

Why Isn't the Effect Taking Effect?

When you drop an effect onto a clip, the clip is sometimes not affected right away because the default settings for the effect are often zero. As soon as you begin making adjustments using the Properties panel, you will start to see changes in the clip.

ADJUSTING THE HUE, LIGHTNESS, OR SATURATION (HLS) IN A CLIP

You can individually adjust the *hue* (which is the color palette of the clip), the *lightness* (the color brightness), or the *saturation* (how intensely the colors are used) of a clip using the Color Balance (HLS) effect. You can adjust just one component of the HLS or any combination; you don't have to make changes to all three.

Start

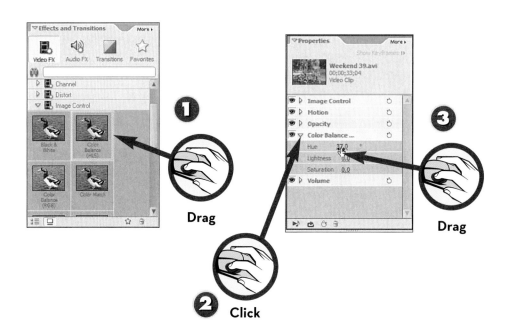

Drag

Drag

Click

① Drag and drop the **Color Balance (HLS)** effect from the **Image Control** folder in the Effects and Transitions panel on to a clip in the Timeline.

② Click the arrow to the left of the **Color Balance (HLS)** effect in the Properties panel to reveal its controls.

③ Drag your mouse to the left or right on the two **Hue** controls to select a new color palette for the clip. You can optionally click the arrow to the right of this control to use the radio dial.

Continued

 TIP

Color TV

Scrolling through the color palettes using the Hue controls is similar to adjusting the color on an old color TV, and as in that process, you might suddenly find that the colors in the clip at last look right to your eye. That's the right time to stop tweaking!

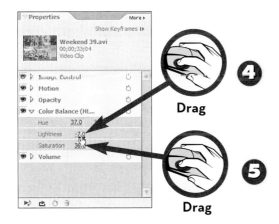

Drag

Drag

Before...

After...

4 Drag your mouse to the left or right on the **Lightness** control to increase or decrease the clip's brightness. You can optionally click the arrow to the right of this control to use the slider control.

5 Drag your mouse to the left or right on the **Saturation** control to increase or decrease the intensity of the colors in the clip. You can optionally click the arrow to the right of this control to use the slider control.

End

TIP
Color Crazy

Conversely, you can use the Color Balance (HLS) effect to create interesting color effects on a clip. You can always cancel any changes by choosing **More**, **Delete Selected Effect**. Or, click the eye next to the effect's name to hide the effect.

ADJUSTING A CLIP'S RED, GREEN, AND BLUE (RGB) LEVELS

You can adjust the levels of any of the three RGB colors—red, blue, and green—using the Color Balance (RGB) effect.

Start

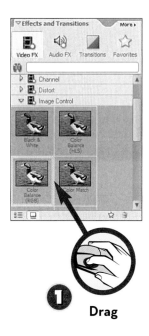

① Drag

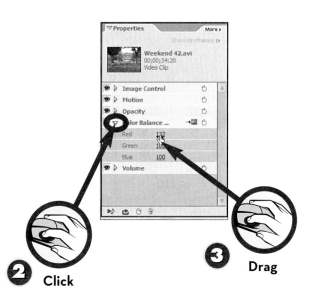

② Click

③ Drag

① Drag and drop the **Color Balance (RGB)** effect from the **Image Control** folder in the Effects and Transitions panel on to a clip in the Timeline.

② Click the arrow to the left of the **Color Balance (RGB)** effect in the Properties panel to reveal its controls.

③ Drag your mouse to the left or right on the **Red** control to increase or decrease the red levels in the clip. You can optionally click the arrow to the right of this control to use the slider control.

Continued

NOTE

Reset It and Forget It

If you've changed an effect and would like to set it back to the default, click the **Reset** button at the bottom of the Properties panel. The **Reset** button looks like an arrow circling back on itself. It's next to the Delete button (the garbage can).

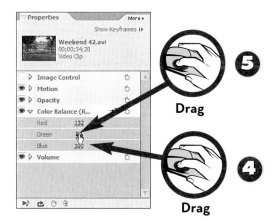

Drag

Drag

Before...

After...

④ Drag your mouse to the left or right on the **Blue** control to increase or decrease the blue levels in the clip. Click the arrow to the right of this control to optionally use the slider control.

⑤ Drag your mouse to the left or right on the **Green** control to increase or decrease the green levels in the clip. Again, click the arrow to the right of this control to optionally use the slider control.

End

TIP

Have a Dialog

To use the dialog box instead of the controls on the Properties panel, click on the dialog box button to the right of the effect's name whenever it's available. Remember to click the **OK** button when you're done.

NOTE

Tint-a-World

The Color Balance (RGB) effect is a great way to tint a clip. Just select any color combination and you can create some interesting tinted effects on your clips. Great for dream sequences, underwater shots, night vision point of view, and so on.

CREATING DRAMATIC COLOR CHANGES WITH THE CHANNEL MIXER

Premiere Elements's Channel Mixer effect gives you control over the various color channels in a video clip, allowing you to tweak a clip until you achieve just the color adjustment or effect that you want.

Start

Drag

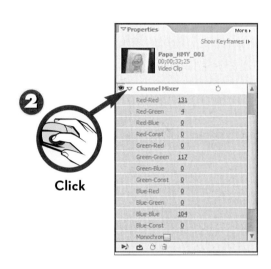

Click

① Drag and drop the **Channel Mixer** effect from the **Adjust** folder in the Effects and Transitions panel to a clip in the Timeline.

② Click the arrow to the left of the **Channel Mixer** effect in the Properties panel to reveal its controls.

Continued

TIP

A Little Mixed Up

It's easy to go a little crazy with the Channel Mixer. Have fun experimenting and use **Undo** or the **Reset** button to return your clip to normal if needed.

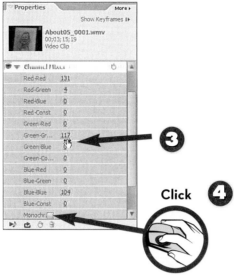

Click ④

Before...

After...

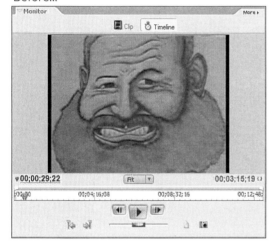

③ Make adjustments as needed to the twelve color areas in the Channel Mixer. Drag your mouse to the left or right on any control to increase or decrease the levels for that color in the clip.

④ To make any clip black and white, click the **Monochrome** check box.

End

NOTE

True Colors

Note that the when the Channel Mixer controls first appear in Properties panel, the RGB colors (red, blue, and green) are all set at 100%. RGB are represented on the Channel Mixer as Red-Red, Green-Green, and Blue-Blue.

ADJUSTING SHADOWS AND HIGHLIGHTS

The Shadow/Highlight effect is especially useful for bringing out the details in a shadowed area in a clip where other parts are in bright sunshine. If you have videotaped a scene and the shadows and highlights aren't right, you can correct them using this filter. You can also use the Shadow/Highlight effect to create interesting moods and special effects.

Start

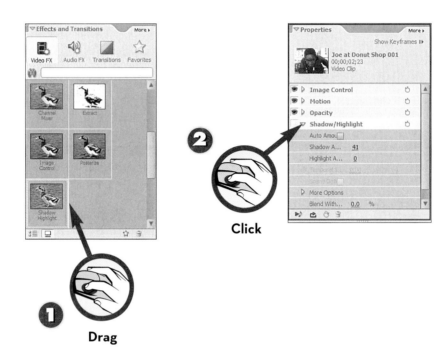

Drag

Click

1. Drag and drop the **Shadow/Highlights** effect from the **Adjust** folder in the Effects and Transitions panel on to a clip in the Timeline.

2. Click the arrow to the left of the **Shadow/Highlights** effect in the Properties panel to reveal its controls.

Continued

NOTE

More Options, More to Like

For this effect, all you need to concentrate on are the two basic settings: Shadow Amount and Highlight Amount. However, if you feel a need to tweak, you'll find that the additional settings under More Options should give you the control you're seeking.

TIP

Automatic Fix

Use Auto Amounts first to see if that works for the clip before you start fine-tuning. Auto Amounts is especially good at fixing clips with backlight problems (such as when the sun is behind the subject).

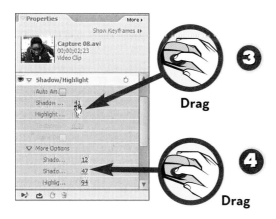

Drag

Drag

Before...

After...

3 Drag the **Shadow** and **Highlight** controls as needed to adjust those settings. You'll see your changes reflected in the Monitor window as you make adjustments.

4 Optionally adjust the settings under More Options as needed.

End

TIP

Avoid the Bleach

The Gamma Correction effect is another way to lighten or darken a clip while leaving the shadows and highlights alone for the most part. However, be aware that the Gamma Correction effect can give you a very bleached-out effect or a very, very darkened look to your clip. If used carefully, this effect might be just what you're looking for. But use with care to avoid startling results—unless, of course, that was just the effect you were looking for!

WORKING WITH THE SOUNDTRACK

The soundtrack of your movie is often one of the most overlooked and neg-lected parts of any project. Yet, it can powerfully transform and enhance your movie with very little effort. The addition of a good song under your entire film can instantly set a mood that is impossible to achieve any other way. Try playing your project with different music playing in the background on your CD player and you'll see a difference with every selection in how you perceive your movie. Happy music makes a fun movie more fun while it can make a seri-ous movie seem absurd. Somber music added to a serious movie can bring you to tears. But your soundtrack is more than just the audio elements you add to it; it's also how you work with those elements.

Premiere Elements includes tools for helping you improve the audio quality on the video and audio clips you are using in your project. You can control how loud or how soft the music plays in your movie, for example, as well as how prominent your narration sounds, if you use one. Tap into the power of audio. Great audio work can make your movie even better, so spend a little extra time thinking about the music you want to use, and how you want to use it. Think of the soundtracks of some of your favorite movies (and even some movies you hated). How was music used in those movies? That can be your model in building your own movies.

ADDING MUSIC, VOICE, AND OTHER SOUNDS TO YOUR MOVIE

You have a world of possibilities above and beyond the noises and conversations that just happened to be around you when you were filming your clips. You can add any number of new audio clips to your soundtrack, and even soften or completely remove the audio in the video clips you took. Don't underestimate the power of audio—or your power to use it!

SETTING A NEW AUDIO-IN (START) POINT

You can set the point at which an audio clip starts, both for a stand-alone audio clip, such as a music track, as well as for the audio portion of a video clip.

Start

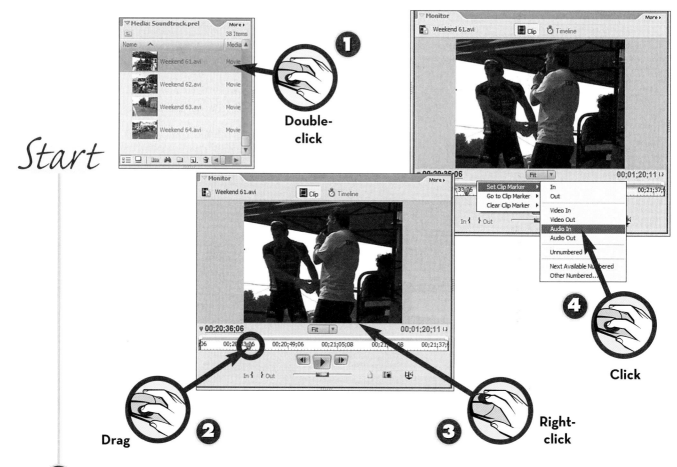

Double-click

Click

Drag ❷

Right-click ❸

❶ Double-click on a clip in the Media panel to view the clip in the Monitor panel.

❷ Move the **CTI** to the point at the start of the clip where you want to set the new audio-in point.

❸ Right-click on the Monitor panel to open the contextual menu.

❹ From the contextual menu, select **Set Clip Marker**, **Audio In**.

End

TIP

Seeing Green

After you insert an audio-in (or audio-out) point, a green audio trim bar appears, showing you the full length of the audio track for this clip. The video track for the clip (if the audio is part of a video clip) appears as a gray trim bar.

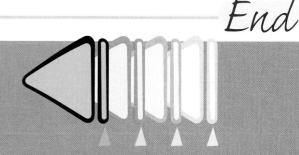

SETTING A NEW AUDIO-OUT (STOP) POINT

You can set the point at which an audio clip ends, both for a stand-alone audio clip, such as a music track, as well as for the audio portion of a video clip.

Start

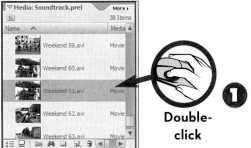

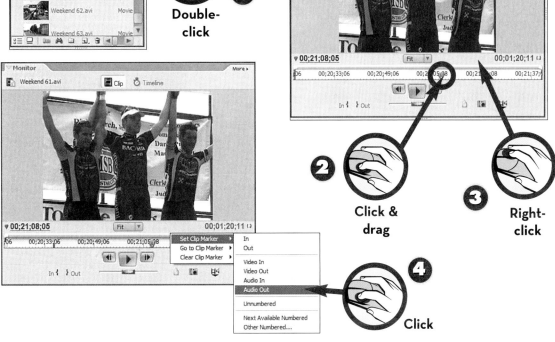

Double-click

Click & drag

Right-click

Click

 Double-click a clip in the Media panel to view it in the Monitor panel.

Move the **CTI** to the point toward the end of the clip where you want to set the new audio-out point.

Right-click on the Monitor panel to open the contextual menu.

From the contextual menu, select **Set Clip Marker**, **Audio Out**.

End

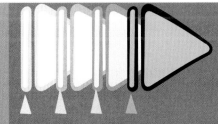

TIP

Adjusting Your Vision

After the "green bar of audio" has made its appearance, you can use your mouse to visually trim the audio-in and audio-out points just as you trim any other media on a timeline. For more information about trimming audio clips, see the following section, "Adjusting the Audio-In and Audio-Out Points."

ADJUSTING THE AUDIO-IN AND AUDIO-OUT POINTS

The audio-in and audio-out points, and thus the length of the audio clip or the audio portion of a video clip, can be easily adjusted using a method known as trimming.

Start

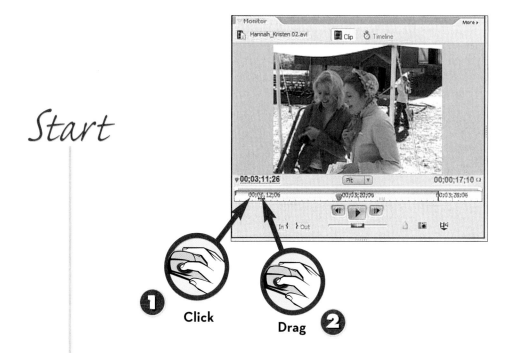

Click

Drag

1 In the time ruler of the Monitor panel, grab one end of the green **audio trim bar** by clicking and holding it. The red and black trim handle appears.

2 Drag the **trim handle** to the left or right to increase or decrease the audio-in or audio-out point.

End

TIP

Accuracy-T-I

To know precisely where you are moving the in or out point, glide the CTI through the clip first and stop at the perfect in or out point. Then go back and grab whichever end of the green bar you need and drag it exactly to the CTI.

ADJUSTING A CLIP'S VOLUME

You can make the audio for a clip louder or softer, or turn it off altogether.

Start

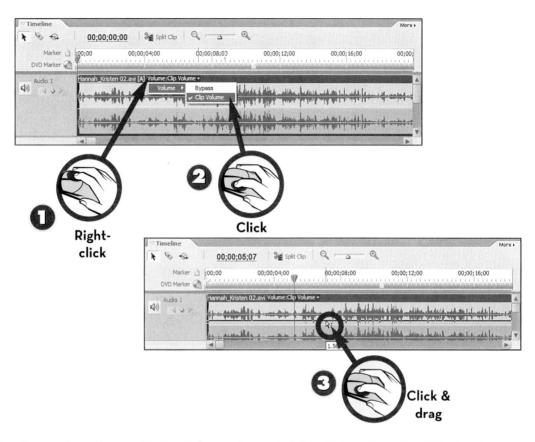

Right-click

Click

Click & drag

1 In the Timeline, select the audio track for a clip and right-click in the clip's title track area (the dark green area at the top of the track) to open the contextual menu.

2 Select **Volume**, **Clip Volume**.

3 Grab the **yellow graph line** (sometimes called a rubber band) and drag it up to increase the clip's volume or drag it down to decrease it.

End

TIP
Sound Off!
To turn a clip's audio completely off, or silent, drag the **yellow graph line** all the way to the bottom, or to 0dB.

TIP
The Volume Effect
You can also adjust the volume using the Volume Audio Effect. For information on using audio effects, see "Using Audio Special Effects," **p. 178**.

SETTING AUDIO GAIN

You can set Audio Gain manually or automatically with Premiere Elements. Audio Gain is similar to volume but refers to the overall strength of the audio signal.

Start

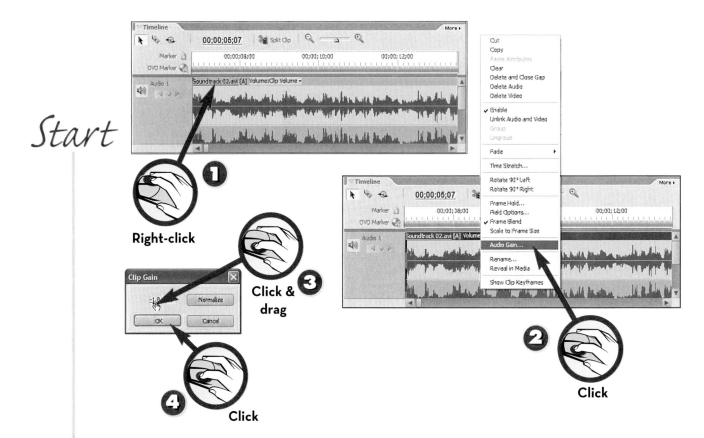

Right-click

Click & drag

Click

Click

1. In the **Timeline**, right-click on the clip whose gain you want to change.

2. Select **Audio Gain**.

3. On the Clip Gain dialog, drag the **dB** field to adjust the gain up or down from the clip's original gain (0.0dB). Move to the left to decrease the gain, and to the right to increase it.

4. Click **OK**.

End

TIP

Gaining Too Much

Be careful when increasing the gain. If the original audio was recorded too low, by increasing the gain you'll hear every pop, squeak, and scratch. A good way to get the gain just right is to use the **Normalize** button on the Clip Gain dialog.

TIP

What's On the Menu

You can access the Clip Gain dialog from the Premiere Elements menu as well. Click on the clip and then select **Clip, Audio Options, Clip Gain**.

USING THE AUDIO METERS TO MONITOR AUDIO LEVELS

Because you record video at different times under different circumstances, and because your audio and video clips can come from different sources, the audio levels (relative loudness, basically) can be different. You can monitor clip loudness using Premiere Elements's Audio Meters panel.

Start

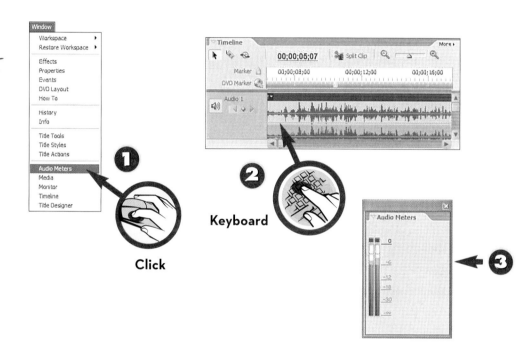

Click

Keyboard

 Select **Window**, **Audio Meters** from the Premiere Elements menu.

 Play the clips on the Timeline by pressing the **Spacebar** on your keyboard.

3 Monitor the Audio Meters panel while the clips play.

End

REMOVING AUDIO FROM A VIDEO CLIP

You can remove the audio from a video clip if you want to replace that audio or simply leave it silent. For example, you might have footage of a busy city street, complete with hurled expletives, screaming sirens, and screeching brakes. You could easily replace all that with a generic sound effect track of more peaceful city noises.

Start

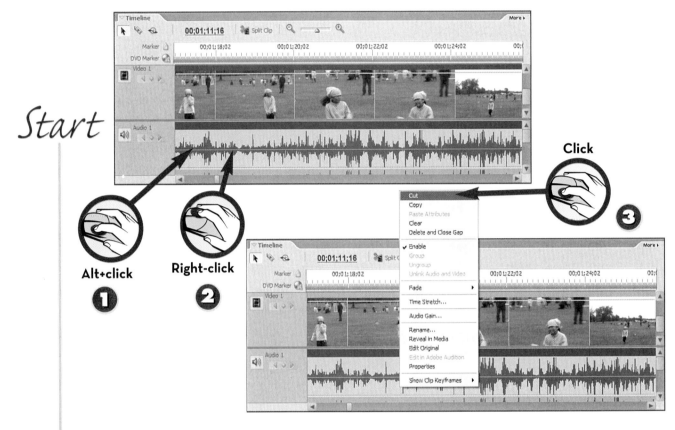

Alt+click   **①**

Right-click   **②**

Click   **③**

① Press the **Alt** key on your keyboard (so only the audio part of the clip will be selected) and click on the **audio clip**. Release the **Alt** key.

② Right-click on the **clip**.

③ From the contextual menu, select **Cut** or **Clear**.

End

 TIP
Not So Drastic Surgery
If you want to shut off the clip's audio and not remove it, you can set the clip's volume to 0dB. Or follow the steps above, but this time select **Enable** from the contextual menu. To turn the audio track back on, click **Enable** again.

TIP
Slide It on Over
When you cut or clear the audio track, the video track stays put. If you want it to slide to the left and fill in any gaps after you delete the audio track, follow the steps above, but this time select **Delete and Close Gap** from the contextual menu.

USING ONLY THE AUDIO PORTION OF A VIDEO CLIP

You might find that you have a great audio track on a video clip, but you don't want to use the video. For example, you might have some great beach noises, with crashing waves and the sounds of laughter, dogs barking, and kids playing. You want to use it as the audio for a scene of a couple sitting at a seaside restaurant where the beach was too far away to hear.

Start

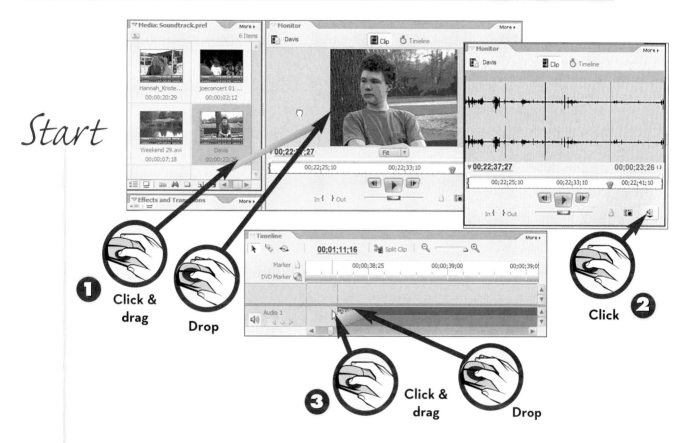

1 Click and drag the clip that you want to use from the Media panel to the Monitor panel.

2 Click the **Take Audio and Video** button until the Take Audio Only option is active (the button looks like a speaker).

3 Click and drag the clip from the **Media panel** to an audio track on the Timeline.

End

ADDING AN AUDIO TRACK AS BACKGROUND MUSIC

It's easy to add an audio track to use as a background music track. After you've added the track below the video, you can adjust the volume as needed to make the music more or less prominent.

Start

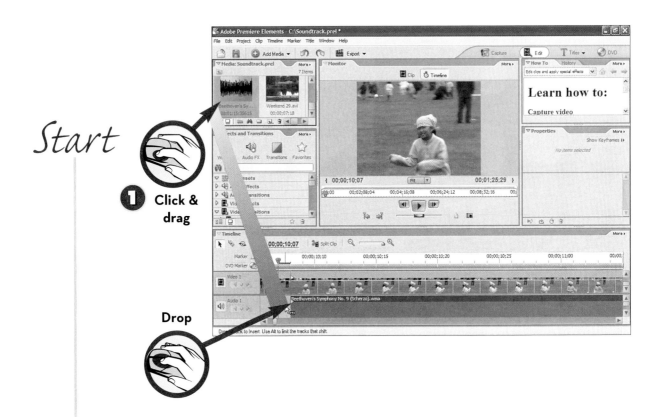

1 Click & drag

Drop

1 Click and drag an audio clip from the Media panel to an empty audio track in the Timeline.

End

TIP

A Little Adjustment

If you prefer, you can open the audio clip in the Monitor panel first to adjust the audio-in and audio-out points before dragging it to the Timeline.

TIP

A Little Light Music

Premiere Elements can't encode music, it can only import it. If you want to use music from your music collection, use Windows Media Player to first create an MP3, WAV, WMA, or AIFF audio file and import it into Premiere Elements using the **Add Media** button.

ADDING A NARRATION TRACK

A good narration can add a lot of value to a video, especially if there is a story associated to the videos you took that might not be fully explained by the video images and sounds alone. It helps to practice a few times. You might even consider writing out your narration first, or at least a cheat sheet of your key points to talk about.

Start

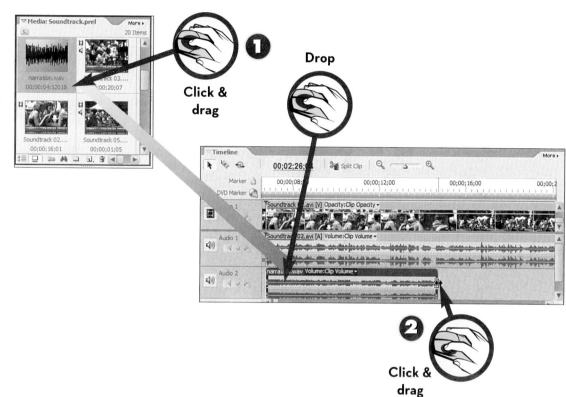

Drop

① **Click & drag**

② **Click & drag**

① Click and drag the **narration** clip to an empty audio track on the Timeline.

② Optionally, adjust the length of the narration clip and the other clips in the project, so the narration syncs with the video.

End

 TIP
Narry a Narration
Premiere Elements can't record a narration track. You'll have to first record your narration using Windows Recorder or a similar application and save it as a WAV file that Premiere Elements can import.

 TIP
Sync or Swim
The best time to record the narration is when your video is almost done. Play your movie, practice narrating to it, and then record your narration. It's also much easier to get the video and audio to sync by recording multiple smaller narration clips.

ADDING A SOUND EFFECT

You can add a sound effect to your project any time you need to. Good sound effects can be found on the Internet or purchased. Your local library might even have a CD or two of good sound effects.

Start

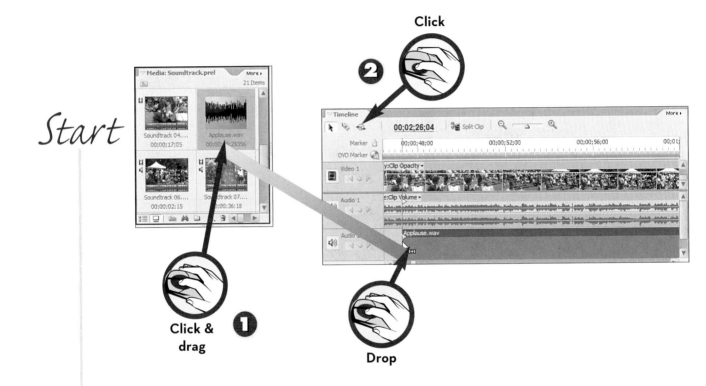

Click

Click & drag **①**

Drop

① Click and drag a sound effect clip from the Media panel to an empty location on an audio track on the Timeline.

② Optionally, adjust the length of the sound effect, its speed (using the Time Stretch tool located on the Timeline), or its location, as needed.

End

TIP

Boing! Bonk! Ker-RASH!
Unless you are deliberately shooting for a Three Stooges feel, be careful not to overdo sound effects. Like special effects and transitions (and spices in cooking), just a little is just enough.

REPLACING A CLIP'S AUDIO TRACK

You might find that you have a great video clip, but the audio just doesn't work. For example, you might have a scene of your family walking along the beach, but all that was recorded on the audio track was the traffic behind you instead of the waves crashing off in the distance and the seagulls overhead. With Premiere Elements, dubbing new audio is easy to do.

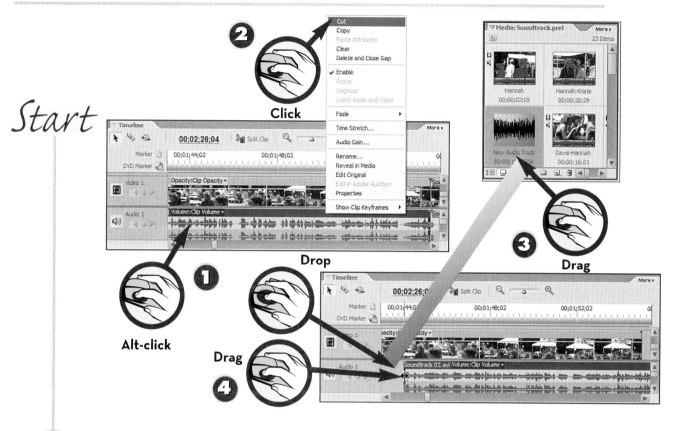

Start

Click

Drop

Drag

Alt-click

Drag

End

1 Remove the original audio track by **Alt+clicking** to select just the audio track.

2 Right-click the audio track and select **Cut**.

3 Drag a new audio track into the place left vacant by the deleted audio track.

4 Optionally, adjust the length of the audio track (or the video track) as needed.

TIP

That Syncing Feeling

Replacing one audio track with another works best with generic clips, where you don't need to synchronize the action with the sounds, such as beach, airport, crowd, or city noises. For example, if you filmed a friend's rock concert, you might get away with overdubbing a studio version of the song along with generic crowd sounds if you used a lot of cut-aways and different shots and angles. It wouldn't work if the performance was "unplugged" with one stationary camera pointed directly at the performer.

USING AUDIO SPECIAL EFFECTS

Premiere Elements includes 17 Audio Effects for improving the quality of the audio you are working with and for adding fun special effects. They are Balance, Bass, Channel Volume, Delay, DeNoiser, Dynamics, Fill Left, Fill Right, Highpass, Invert, Lowpass, Notch, PitchShifter, Reverb, Swap Channels, Treble, and Volume.

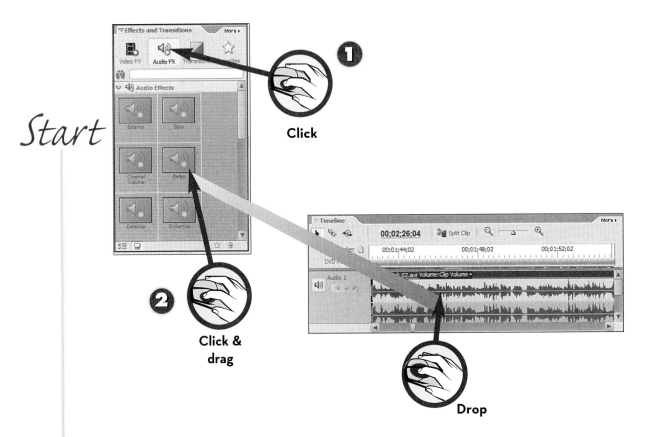

Start

Click

Click & drag

Drop

1 Click the **Audio FX** button on the Effects and Transitions panel.

2 Click and drag one of the audio effects to an audio clip on the Timeline.

Continued

TIP

Sick and Sassy

Although audio effects can repair problems with audio files (such as the Notch effect eliminating an annoying hum), these effects are also a great way to enhance audio tracks by adjusting the treble or bass or changing the balance. They can also be great fun. For example, you can use the PitchShifter's Cartoon Mouse effect to give someone a very high-sounding voice, or the Delay filter to add an echo. Use the Reverb effect to make it seem as if two people are talking in an empty church or large hall.

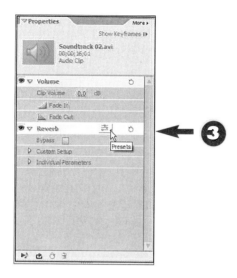

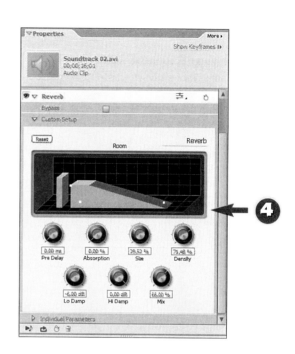

3 Optionally, adjust the settings for the audio effect in the **Properties panel**.

4 When available, use the photo-realistic controls to further adjust the audio effect.

End

TIP

(Almost) Like the Real Thing

Although audio effects use controls you might already be familiar with, some also use 3D dials you can turn almost as if you were at a console in a studio. Denoiser, Dynamics, Reverb, and PitchShifter all have these dials available under **Custom Settings**.

USING AUDIO TRANSITIONS

Premiere Elements includes two Audio Crossfade Transitions: Constant Gain and Constant Power. When applied to the beginning of a clip, the audio fades in, and when applied to the end of a clip, the audio fades out. You can have an audio transition at both the beginning and end of the same clip.

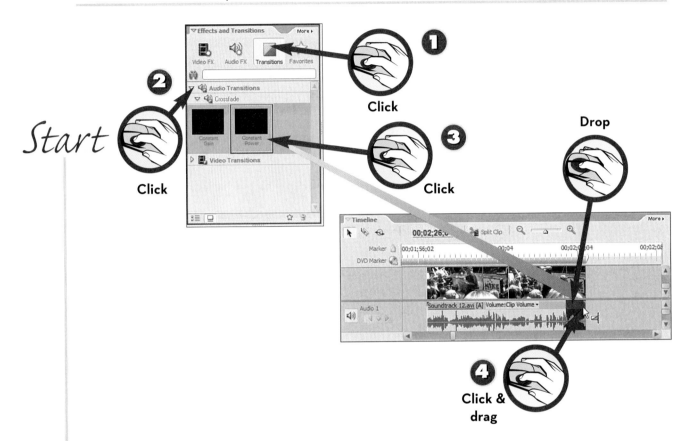

Start

1 Click the **Transitions** button on the Effects and Transitions panel.

2 Click the triangle next to **Audio Transitions** to open it and select **Crossfade**.

3 Select either **Constant Gain** or **Constant Power**.

4 Click and drag the transition onto an audio clip in the **Timeline**.

Continued

TIP
Untouchable
Audio clips don't need to be touching in order to have an audio transition applied. The clip uses the transition on the way in and on the way out regardless of whether another clip led into it first or is starting next.

Click

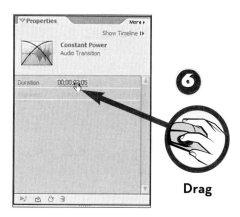

Drag

5 To make additional adjustments, click on the effect's name on the audio clip.

6 Optionally, adjust the **Duration** in the Properties panel by dragging left or right in the number field.

End

TIP

Purple Haze

As you hover the transition over an audio clip looking for the right place to drop it, the clip highlights at either the front or the back (head or tail) in deep purple to let you know at which end you are. In addition, the cursor changes to a flag, pointing to the right to indicate that you're at the head of a clip, and to the left to indicate that you're at the tail. After you drop the transition where you want it, the audio transition appears as a light and dark purple rectangle on the label area of the audio clip.

SHARING YOUR MOVIE WITH FRIENDS AND FAMILY

This is what you have waited for, what you have worked so hard to achieve: getting your movie out of Premiere Elements and to your public! Whether that public eagerly awaits somewhere on the Internet, at the other end of an email address, over your shoulder at your computer, or at your television or home theater by way of your latest DVD, you want to share with them the results of your hard work and creative vision.

Premiere Elements has a complete set of templates which you can use to build your DVD menus. There are designs for sports themes, entertainment themes, new baby themes, as well as education, seasons, travel, and wedding themes. Want to create a DVD with no menus at all that simply starts playing as soon as you put the disc in your DVD drive? No problem: Premiere Elements can do that, too.

Premiere Elements has full support for DVD, giving you the ability to create DVD menus, submenus, and motion menus—those little buttons on the DVD menu that loop actual video clips from your movie. Premiere Elements also supports the major video formats—Windows Media (AVI), QuickTime (.MOV), and MPEG (MPG)—in a variety of sizes and resolutions. Each of these sizes and resolutions are ideally suited for email, Internet dialup connections, and Internet broadband (such as cable and DSL). With all of these movie-finishing capabilities, Premiere Elements is a full soup-to-nuts video-editing solution.

CREATING VIDEO FILES AND DVDS

It's time to finish your movie and share it with your friends and family! With Premiere Elements, you can save your movie to a number of file formats, burn directly to a DVD or Video CD, or record it back to tape—no matter which option you choose, you'll be able to premiere your movie!

CREATING DVD MENUS

Premiere Elements has tools for creating sophisticated DVD menus for your movies. You can use the built-in templates or create a DVD that automatically plays as soon as you pop it in your DVD player.

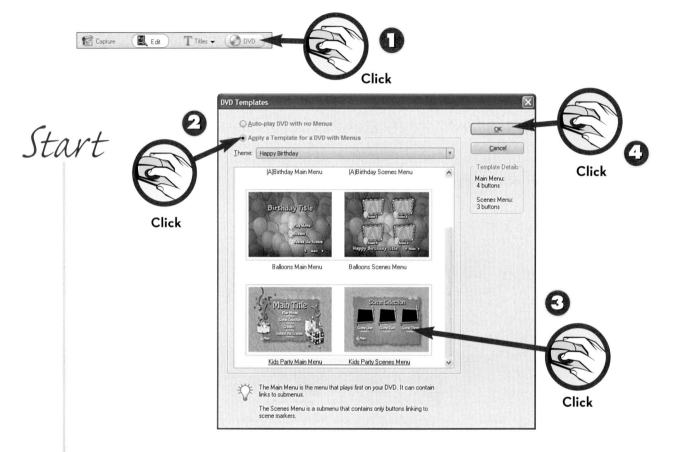

Start

Click

1 Click the **DVD** button.

2 To create menus for your DVD, select **Apply a Template for a DVD with Menus**.

3 Select one of Premiere Elements's DVD menu templates.

4 Click **OK**.

Continued

Continued

NOTE

More Than It Themes

Be sure to check out all of the themes available under the Themes drop-down list. There are themes with multiple designs in a variety of categories including weddings, sports, and birthdays.

TIP

No Menus, No Problem

To create a DVD that automatically plays when inserted into a DVD player, make sure **Auto-Play DVD with No Menus** is selected.

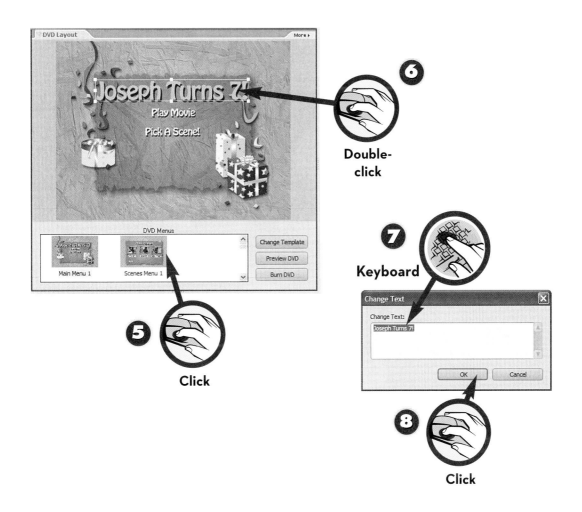

5 Click on one of the small views at the bottom of the DVD Layout panel to switch to it.

6 Change text for any element by double-clicking on a text block in the large window.

7 In the Change Text window, change the text.

8 When you're done, click **OK**.

End

TIP

Check It Out

Use the Preview DVD button to see what your DVD will look like and how it will behave. To select a different template, select the **Change Template** button. You can even burn your DVD disc directly from the DVD Layout panel by selecting the **Burn DVD** button.

USING DVD SCENE MARKERS

Premiere Elements gives you complete control over DVD markers in the DVD menus for your disc, letting you create as sophisticated and as wild a DVD as you want.

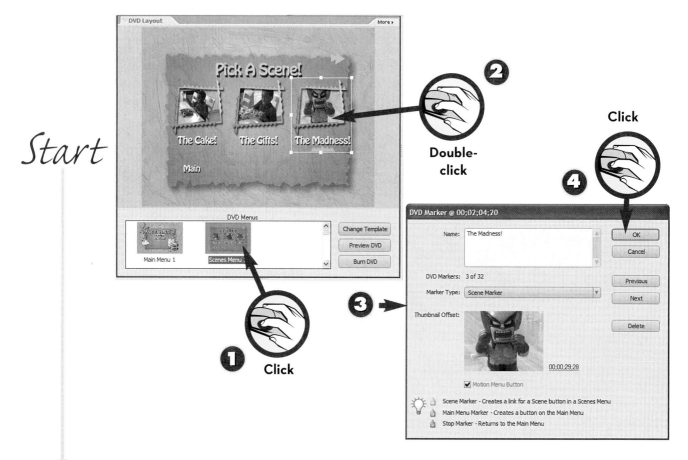

Start

1 On the DVD Layout panel, click on a **Scenes Menu** icon to view it.

2 Double-click on a scene to open the DVD Marker panel.

3 Make changes to the name, select a new marker, set the marker as a Motion Menu Button, select a new thumbnail, change the marker type, or delete the marker all together.

4 When you're done, click **OK**.

End

NOTE

Missing Markers

DVD markers along the Timeline indicate where you want a scene to begin. Premiere Elements uses these markers to automatically create menu buttons. If you didn't use DVD markers, you'll see a pop up offering a quick solution. If you don't like the solution, you can move the DVD markers on the Timeline to exactly where you want them. Or use the **More** button on the DVD Layout panel to regenerate the DVD markers as needed.

CUSTOMIZING THE DVD BACKGROUND

You can customize the background of your DVD menus with any background you want. It can be a still image (photograph), or it can be a video clip that Premiere Elements will show in motion.

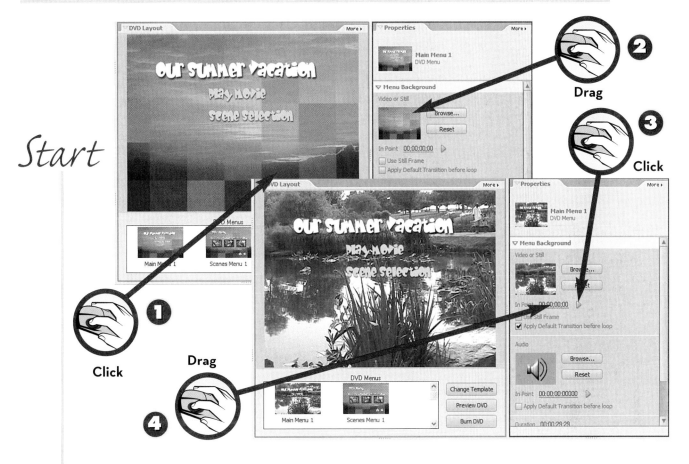

Start

Click

Drag

Click

Drag

1 Click the background of any menu in the DVD Layout panel.

2 Drag and drop a new still or video from the Media panel onto the Video or Still area of the Properties panel or use the **Browse** button to select the file.

3 Click the green triangle to play the clip if it's a video clip.

4 Drag the **In Point** to select the in, or starting, point for the clip.

End

TIP

Other Options

You can select **Use Still Frame** to use only a frame from a video. You can also choose to use Premiere Elements's default transition with a clip by selecting the **Apply Default Transition Before Loop** check box.

CUSTOMIZE DVD MENUS

After you have selected a DVD template to use in Premiere Elements, you can change any element on the screen: the background, the menu graphics, and any and all of the text.

Click

Start

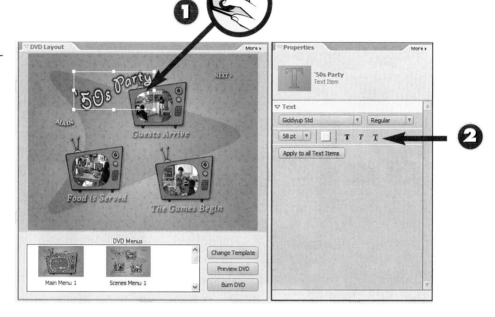

After you have a DVD template loaded in the DVD Layout panel, click on any element to see its properties display in the Properties panel.

For text elements, you can adjust properties such as font, font color, and font size.

Continued

 **TIP**
One for All
If you want to apply your changes to not just the text element you selected but to all text, click **Apply to All Text Items**.

 TIP
That's More Like It
Don't forget about the **More** button. Here, it gives you an alternate way to access the panel's three buttons (Preview DVD, Change Template, and Burn DVD), and to auto-generate DVD markers. But more importantly, it enables you to turn on safe margins, which is a good idea if you are modifying the templates significantly.

Click

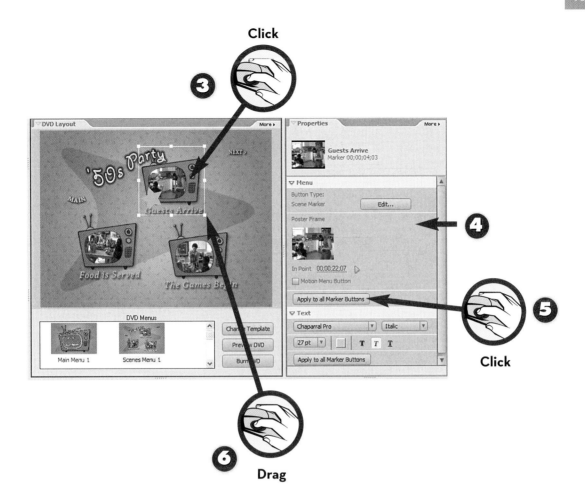

Drag

Click

3 Select a graphic element such as a Marker button.

4 Optionally change the settings such as the poster frame, the font, the font color, and so on.

5 Apply your changes to all Marker buttons by clicking the **Apply to All Marker Buttons** button.

6 Move or resize the graphic as needed.

End

TIP

Background in Motion

The background and any of the menu buttons can be motion menus. That is, instead of being a still image, you can optionally use video or animation clips that can loop in the menu button until clicked. You can have all of the buttons be in motion, or just one or some of the buttons. To make an element a motion menu, just click the **Motion Menu Button** check box when it's available.

BURNING YOUR MOVIE TO A DVD

Burning to a DVD is a straightforward procedure with Premiere Elements. You need to set up your DVD burner one time and you're ready to go.

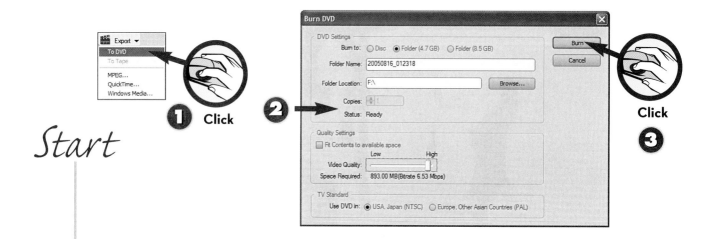

Start

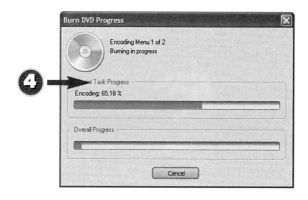

1 Click the **Export** button and choose **To DVD**.

2 Select the settings you want, such as whether to burn directly to disc or to a folder on your computer or network; number of copies; video quality (low to high); and so on.

3 Click **Burn**.

4 The Burn DVD Progress window keeps you informed of how things are going.

End

NOTE

Don't Get Burned

Burning DVDs is trickier than it looks. Keep a few things in mind and you'll have success. First, defragment your hard drive. Close all other running programs except for Premiere Elements. Disconnect from the Internet if you're connected and then shut down your virus protection software. Don't try to burn a movie more than a half an hour or so in length. Finally, burn slow but burn steady.

SAVING YOUR MOVIE TO A VIDEO FILE

With Premiere Elements you can save your amazing movie to a number of format files for distribution in a number of ways. Premiere Elements has settings for automatically creating the right type of file for sending via email, for being viewed by Internet users who connect using a dialup modem, or to be viewed by Internet users connected by a broadband (DLS or cable) modem. You can even create a VCD file to burn to a CD for watching on a DVD player (the quality is about the same as VHS) or create files to play on mobile phones!

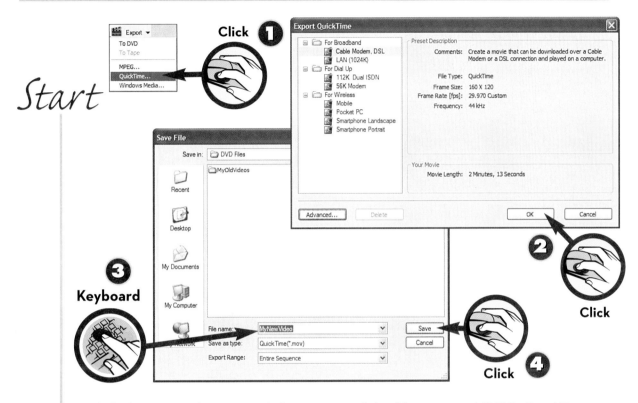

Start

Keyboard

Click

Click

Click

End

1. Click the **Export** button and choose one of the file options: MPEG, QuickTime, or Windows Media.

2. Select the file type based on use (broadband, dial up, or wireless) and associated details. Modify the settings on the Export window and click **OK**.

3. Give the file a name on the Save File dialog.

4. Click **Save** and Premiere Elements renders the file and saves it.

NOTE

Proper Behavior

The Export Settings window is especially good for one thing: automatically selecting the right settings for modem uploads, email, and so on. For QuickTime and Windows Media (but not for MPEG), at the top of the Export Settings window you can select from a list of export options to find just the format situation for which you're looking.

CREATING A VCD DISC

With Premiere Elements, you can even create a VCD file to burn to a CD for watching on a DVD player. VCD stands for *Video CD* and works just like a DVD, but with a video quality about the same as VHS tape (about half that of a DVD). Premiere Elements doesn't burn a VCD, but you create the VCD file with Premiere Elements and then just copy it to a CD. VCD discs will play in many newer DVD players.

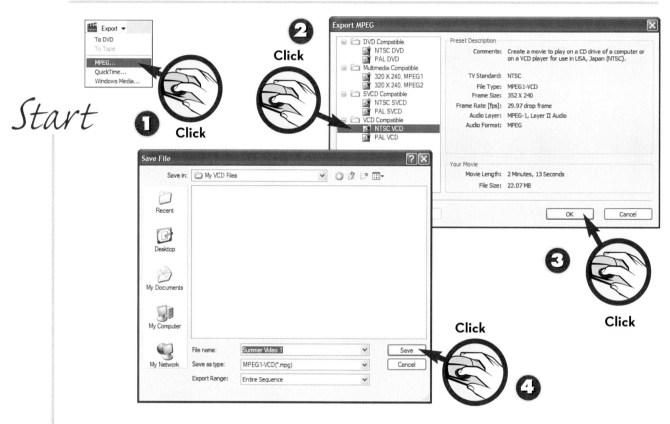

Start

1. Click the **Export** button and choose **MPEG**.

2. Click **NTSC VCD** under VCD Compatible. (Outside the United States, you might need to choose PAL VCD.)

3. Click **OK**.

4. Give the file a name and click **Save**. Premiere Elements renders the file and saves it.

End

SAVING YOUR MOVIE TO TAPE

If you don't have a DVD or CD burner, you can save your movie back to your digital camcorder using a FireWire connection. You can then view your video by connecting your camcorder to your TV using RCA connectors or recording from your camcorder to a VCR.

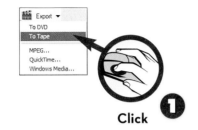

Click

Start

Click

1 Click the **Export** button and choose **To Tape**.

2 Modify the settings on the Export to Tape window, such as whether to delay the movie start slightly or to preroll the tape a frame or two.

3 Click **Record**.

End

A

analog video (AV)   Video used by a TV, VCR, and analog camcorder. Before analog video can be edited on a computer, it must be converted to a computer-readable format. See also **digital video (DV)**.

aspect ratio   The ratio of height (H) to width (W) of the TV picture. For a standard TV or monitor, the aspect ratio is 4:3. For HDTV (High Definition TV), it's 16:9.

Audio Gain   See **gain**.

B

blue screen   A blue cloth or background against which an actor performs. The blue is later dropped out and replaced with a video background. The effect is also called bluescreening, greenscreening (green is also used), and chromakeying.

C

capture   To bring video in from a camcorder, VCR, or other source into a computer.

chrominance   The color part of a video signal that contains information on a color's hue (the color itself, such as blue) and saturation (whether it's pale blue or navy blue).

clip   Any single piece of media that has its own start point and end point which can be cut, copied, moved, or otherwise treated individually either in the Timeline or in the Monitor panel.

CODEC   A technology for compressing and decompressing images and sound. CODECs define the video settings such as the frame rate and size. Some of the more popular CODECs are MPEG-2, WMV (Windows Media), DivX, and QuickTime.

Current Time Indicator (CTI)   The device that looks like a thin wire with a blue guitar pick on top attached to the Timeline in Premiere Elements. The CTI flows along the Timeline at the current time (thus the name, Current Time Indicator). Sometimes referred to as the scrubber by video editors because you can also grab the CTI to scrub along the Timeline.

cut   A clip can be cut at a given point to create two new clips. Any clip can be cut.

D

digital video (DV)   Format that allows a digital signal to be captured on tape. Unlike analog video, the video is ready to be edited on a computer and requires no conversion because the information is already digital (ones and zeros). See also **analog video (AV)**.

digitize   When video is digitized, analog video (from videotape) is converted into a computer-readable format.

Dissolve   A type of transition where the first clip dissolves or breaks apart in some way to reveal the next clip.

E

effects (FX)   Any change applied to a video clip to alter its appearance or shape is called an effect or sometimes a special effect.

Effects and Transitions panel   Holds the full list of available effects and transitions in Premiere Elements, both audio and video, as well as Presets.

F

fade   A type of transition where one clip fades out as the next scene fades in. The fade can be a gradual fade to transparency. There is also a fade to black and a fade up from black, both of which are a well-known part of the filmmaker's toolkit. Premiere Elements includes a number of transitions in the fade category. See also **transition**.

final cut   The final version of the movie, ready to be burned to DVD or otherwise prepared for distribution or sharing. Similar to a writer's final draft of a story. See also **rough cut**.

FireWire   Apple Computer's name for the technology for transferring digital video. Also known as FireWire 400, FireWire 800, or IEEE 1394.

footage   Because film is traditionally measured in feet, what you shoot is called footage. See also **raw footage**.

fps   Frames per second. This is the measuring system for video and movies. The standard rate is 30fps. Movies prepared for viewing over the Internet are typically saved at 10–15fps for faster downloading.

frame   A single still picture in a video. To simulate real life, movies play back 30 frames per second (fps). The eye and brain mentally fit them together to create the illusion of movement, action, and life.

G

gain   The audio level of the clip. You can increase or decrease a clip's gain as needed to give all the clips in a movie the same level of audio.

GPU   Graphics processing unit. Graphics cards that support Direct 3D (among other things) allow the use the GPU effects in Premiere Elements, such as Page Curl and Card Flip.

green screen   See **blue screen**.

H

HDTV   High Definition Television. HDTV is a set of standards for television broadcast and display that increases picture definition to 720 or 1080 lines, resulting in a cleaner, clearer video image.

head   The very start of a clip. See also **tail**.

hue   Refers to the color in a clip. Hue is simply another name for color.

I

IEEE 1394   See **FireWire**.

inserting   When you insert a clip in the Timeline, the clips on either side are shifted out of the way. No video is lost from any clip and the movie's overall time is increased by the length of the new clip. See also **overlay**.

Iris   One of the many types of transitions available with Premiere Elements. This transition changes from clip A to clip B simulating the closing or opening of a camera iris. See also **transition**.

J

J-cut   A type of split edit. The term *J-cut* refers to how the altered shape of the audio and video of the clip looks like the capital letter *J*. With a J-cut, the audio from the next clip is heard before you see the its video while the preceding clip is playing. See also **L-cut**.

JPEG   Joint Photographic Experts Group. An industry standard for compressing images while maintaining image quality. JPEG allows for increasingly smaller file sizes, as needed, with subsequent subtle losses in picture quality.

K

keyframes Individual frames in a clip where something key happens in an effect, especially a motion effect, such as a stop point or a turning point.

L

L-cut Another type of split edit, the other being the J-cut. Both involve how the audio track of one clip is heard at either the beginning or end of a second clip. With an L-cut, the audio from the preceding clip is heard while you are viewing the next clip's video. See also **J-cut**.

letterbox Letterbox, or widescreen, is a format with an aspect ratio similar to a movie screen.

linear editing See **nonlinear editing (NLE)**.

luminance The part of a video signal that carries information about the brightness of the video picture. See also **chrominance**.

M

Marker Used throughout Premiere Elements as a way to set placeholders as you work. You can set numbered, unnumbered, and DVD Markers in Premiere Elements.

media Any acceptable file that can be added to the Media panel in Premiere Elements and subsequently used on the Timeline to build a movie. Media includes video clips, pictures, drawings, music, narration, sound effects, and titles.

Media panel Where you collect media clips. You can also create folders and subfolders in the Media panel to help organize media, such as a Music folder or a Photos folder.

Motion Effect An effect where you are setting a clip in motion, typically where a clip flies in from one side of the screen to stop on the other side, or where a clip flips or tumbles across the screen.

MPEG Moving Picture Experts Group. An industry standard for compressing video (movie) files while still maintaining a high level of video quality. There are several types of MPEG, but the most popular are MPEG-1 (used for video CDs and MP3s) and MPEG-2 (used for digital video, DVDs, and HDTV).

N

nonlinear editing (NLE) Before computer editing, movies and video were edited linearly, that is, in a line. Tape was loaded into a machine and played from beginning to end. Edits were made using a razor and tape to splice together the finished film. With computers, movies are now edited nonlinearly; that is, in a random order.

Glossary

NTSC National Television Standards Committee. The national organization in the United States that sets the television and broadcast standards so all televisions, videotapes, VCRs, DVDs, and DVD players are compatible. NTSC video is compatible in the United States, Canada, and Japan. See also **PAL**.

O

overlay Overlaying a clip onto the Timeline overwrites whatever clip or clip section is already sitting at that point on the Timeline, erasing it. The overall length of the movie is not increased at all. See also **inserting**.

overscan The television signal is slightly overscanned, or enlarged, when the image is broadcast and viewed. This results in any images or text around the very outside edges being pushed out of sight. Premiere Elements enables you to see the safe areas on the screen as you work, especially with titles.

P

PAL Phase Alternate Line. The video standard in most of Europe. (France, Eastern Europe, and parts of Africa use a standard known as SECAM.) PAL is just enough different from NTSC to make it incompatible. In other words, a videotape recorded in PAL won't play on a U.S.-made VCR. See also **NTSC**.

panning Moving across a scene from left to right or top to bottom. Premiere Elements can simulate this effect on a video clip or a photograph with any of the available Pan Effects. Sometimes referred to as the Ken Burns Effect. See also **zoom**.

PiP Picture-in-Picture. The technique of placing one video within another. You can have one PiP or many PiPs on the screen at one time.

pixel From *picture element*. Refers to the smallest element on a computer screen or in a computer image. Each picture on a computer, including the individual frames of a video, is made up of pixels.

previewing To watch a clip in the Monitor panel. (You can also preview a clip in the Preview Area in the Media panel.) When you add an effect, transition, or title to a project, you are seeing a real time preview version of it until you render it. The preview is a close approximation of how that effect, transition, or title will look after it's rendered.

project   Each movie you work on in Premiere Elements is set up in what is called a project. Everything needed to create a movie is brought into the project. Project files have the extension **.prel**.

Properties panel   The advanced effects panel for Premiere Elements where you control the settings for an effect, set keyframes for motion effects, and so on.

Q

QuickTime   The multimedia technology and flexible media player developed by Apple Computer, Inc. for creating and storing sound, graphics, and video files. Though originally a Macintosh technology, QuickTime now runs equally well on Windows PCs.

R

raw footage   Any video you took that has not yet been altered or trimmed in Premiere Elements.

real time   Premiere Elements can show what any effect, transition, or title looks like in a project as soon as you select it. You are really seeing an estimation in a preview mode, so in some cases it might run slightly slower than when it's fully rendered. See also **rendering**.

rendering   The process by which Premiere Elements applies effects, transitions, or titles to video clips. Until you render, what you are viewing is a real time preview.

rough cut   The initial assembly of clips to create the movie. Similar to a writer's first draft of a story. See also **final cut**.

S

saturation   The amount of color in a given clip. Colors in a clip with too high a degree of saturation appear very rich, or oversaturated; colors with too low a degree of saturation appear washed out, or undersaturated. See also **chrominance**.

scrub   To move through a clip or movie back and forth at varying speeds, usually to find a particular scene or frame in the movie or clip. In Premiere Elements, you scrub using the CTI (the Current Time Indicator).

scrubber   See **Current Time Indicator (CTI)**.

shuttle Sometimes called the jog shuttle, this is a small device on the interface of the Media panel in Premiere Elements that enables you to move, or scrub, back and forth through a clip. The shuttle is a reference to the jog shuttle device found on video-editing equipment.

SMPTE Society of Motion Picture and Television Engineers. This group defines the standards used in video production, similar to how ANSI sets standards for computers and software.

split edit A type of edit where the audio and video parts of a clip are trimmed separately. See also **J-cut** and **L-cut**.

split screen When two clips share the screen at the same time, usually at 50%, and with the screen divided in the middle vertically or horizontally.

storyboard In movies, a hand-drawn or computer-drawn sketch of every scene in a movie before it is filmed. In Premiere Elements, a way of using the Media panel to arrange clips before adding them to the Timeline.

superimposing A technique of layering one video clip or title clip over another video clip with transparency. The underlying clip shows through to some degree, allowing for the creation of a number of interesting effects.

T

tail The very end of a clip. See also **head**.

timecode A timecode is attached to every video clip that comes into Premiere Elements as well as to the full movie in the Timeline. The timecode is in the format HH;MM;SS;FF and it tells where you are in the clip or movie in terms of hours, minutes, seconds, and frames.

Timeline The wide, horizontal panel that sits at the bottom of the Premiere Elements workspace. The Timeline graphically represents the duration of the movie, from beginning to end, running from left to right.

title Any kind of text that appears in a movie. Typically a title displays at the beginning of a movie and tells the name of the movie. Titles are also used as credits at the end of a film. Titles can also be used to identify who's speaking or where a scene is taking place.

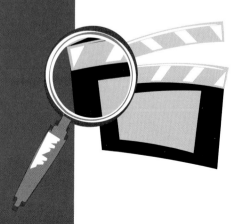

Title Designer   Where titles are created, including rolling and scrolling titles. Premiere Elements ships with a number of templates that can be used as the starting point.

transition   An effect between two clips that is used to ease the transition between the clips. Transitions are best used to delineate a change in time or setting. Transitions include 3-D Motion, Dissolves, Peels, Wipes, and Zooms, among others.

trimming   The act of shortening a clip's length, either from the beginning or from the end. When you trim a clip you are actually only hiding the video and audio that you trim; you are not cutting it away.

U-V

USB   Universal Serial Bus. Used to attach printers, keyboards, external hard drives, and so on, to a computer.

W-X-Y-Z

waveform   A graphical representation of an audio signal. Premiere Elements shows the waveform for audio clips in the Monitor panel.

Wipe   A type of transition where one clip wipes across the screen to reveal the next clip.

workspace   The main work area in Premiere Elements, where all the panels are laid out. Premiere Elements actually has a number of workspaces depending upon the task at hand, such as editing, creating titles, or burning a DVD.

zoom   There are a number of ways to zoom in Premiere Elements. You can zoom in or out on a clip using the Zoom effect; zoom in or out on the Media panel to get a closer, more detailed look at a clip; or zoom in or out on the Timeline, to show more or less of the project as you work on it.

Zoom Transition   A type of transition that simulates one clip zooming in or out to reveal the next clip.

C

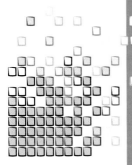

F

G – H – I

Index

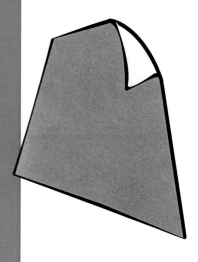

N - O - P

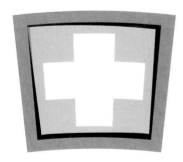

Index